COFFIN CORNER BOYS

One Bomber, Ten Men, and Their Harrowing Escape from Nazi-Occupied France

CAROLE ENGLE AVRIETT

with **CAPT. GEORGE W. STARKS**
WWII B-17 Pilot, the Mighty Eighth
Foreword by **LT. GEN. E. G. "BUCK" SHULER JR.**
Former Commander, Eighth Air Force

**REGNERY
HISTORY**
Washington, D.C.

Regnery History™ is a trademark of Salem Communications Holding Corporation
Regnery® is a registered trademark and its colophon is a trademark of Salem Communications Holding Corporation

Cataloging-in-Publication data on file with the Library of Congress

ISBN: 978-1-68451-192-1

Library of Congress Control Number: 2017034247

First trade paperback edition published 2021

Published in the United States by
Regnery History
An imprint of Regnery Publishing
A Division of Salem Media Group
Washington, D.C.
www.RegneryHistory.com

Manufactured in the United States of America

10 9 8 7 6 5 4 3 2 1

Books are available in quantity for promotional or premium use. For information on discounts and terms, please visit our website: www.RegneryHistory.com.

I dedicate this book...to the nine men in my crew; they were the very best. And...to the French "helpers," especially Maurice Baverel, the gutsiest man I ever met.

—Dr. George Wiley Starks

CONTENTS

PART VI FINDING OLD FRIENDS

FOREWORD

Lieutenant General
E. G. "Buck" Shuler Jr., USAF (Ret).

I am honored to have been asked to pen the foreword for *Coffin Corner Boys*, a remarkable narrative about Dr. George W. Starks and his B-17 crew assigned to the Ninety-Second Bomb Group of the Eighth Air Force during World War II. I have known George Starks for nearly fifteen years, when he became an early supporter of the National Museum of the Mighty Eighth Air Force, and we served on the board of trustees together.

What I did not know was the details of his distinguished military service as a B-17 pilot during the heavy combat operations of the Second World War. With the privilege of reading the working manuscript detailing the first-person accounts by George and his crew members of their shoot-down on March 16, 1944, by FW-190 fighters, I became aware of their grueling experiences. The reader of this book will become immersed in the experience of flying combat in a B-17, facing the terrible dangers and dilemmas of their mission, and then being forced to save themselves from death.

Each crew member's account of that fateful day is absolutely fascinating! Although this is one of hundreds of such stories to come out of the Eighth Air Force's combat operations, it is unique to George and his crew. Clearly, this young crew, with an average age of only twenty-two, conducted itself in a highly professional manner, exhibiting tremendous courage under the most difficult of circumstances.

I would be remiss if I did not commend George for not only sharing this story but for including the stories of the French "helpers" who provided aid once the crew was on the ground, as well as his efforts to keep the crew in touch with one another after the war.

Additionally, George was a great help to me in my role as chairman of the board and CEO as we put together the National Museum of the Mighty Eighth Air Force. I will be forever grateful for his many ideas and support of the museum while serving on the board. During my service as the commander of the Eighth Air Force and my responsibilities with the museum, I really got to know so many Eighth Air Force veterans of World War II. My respect for their service and sacrifice is unbounded.

On a personal note, America entered the war on the day after my fifth birthday. At the time, my family was living in Caracas, Venezuela, where my dad was a civil engineer with Creole Petroleum Corporation, building roads back in the oil fields. I recall vividly how deeply concerned my parents were upon learning of the attack on Pearl Harbor. They piled brother Jake and me into the Chevy and drove to the American embassy to meet with Ambassador Corrigan to find out just what was happening to our nation.

The family soon returned to South Carolina, where we settled in while dad spent two years in the Pacific with the Navy Seabees building airfields. He would make the invasion of the Marshall Islands and supervise the construction of an airfield on Majuro. Later he would serve on the island commander's staff on Tinian in the Marianas Islands. Although very young, I was keenly aware of what was going on. I am certain that the events of WWII served as the genesis of my desire to serve in the military, which began with my commissioning at the Citadel on June 6, 1959, the fifteenth anniversary of the D-Day invasion.

My exposure to the "Greatest Generation" of Eighth Air Force veterans has often caused me to wish that I had been able to fly and fight with them! Enjoy the read.

E. G. "Buck" Shuler Jr.
Lieutenant General, USAF, Retired
Former Commander Eighth Air Force
March 1988 to May 1992

REMEMBRANCES

By Paul and Mike Starks

Paul Starks

I grew up hearing the stories from Dad: lost over the Atlantic, bailing out of the airplane right before it exploded, coming face to face with German soldiers, running across the border after the border guards had passed, and more.

Dad had been back several times over the years, but he talked about going again one more time before he got too old, and he wanted me to go with him. He was ninety-two, and he and I determined we had to make the time.

We arrived in France in the early morning, rented a car, and drove several hours to a small town near our starting point to retrace my dad's escape route from the Germans in occupied France. Both of us were filled with anticipation and excitement.

After renting a motel room we began to look for the place he landed in the parachute near Vitry-en-Perthois. We visited the farm where the plane had crashed and later commenced retracing the route toward Switzerland. We found places he had not seen for a long time, and finally the very spot where he ran across the border to freedom.

Sometimes it was hard to watch him reminisce. It was difficult to imagine what was going through his mind after a whole lifetime, but it was touching to see his reaction.

On a larger scale, I am in awe of the men—no, they were just boys—many of whom had never been away from home until they climbed inside a paper-thin aluminum skin and went off to vicious combat in such an unrelenting, hostile environment. And then do it again the next day. I can't imagine the fortitude it took. They inspired me to become a student of the air war during WWII and especially the Eighth Air Force. I am honored and proud to have seen what my dad did.

Mike Starks

I was thirteen when Dad called Paul and me together and told us he was going back to France and then elk hunting in Wyoming. He said one of us could go on each trip and left it to us to decide. It was one of the few times there was no disagreement. I immediately said, "France" and Paul said, "elk hunting." And so it was.

I have always been a history buff and looked forward to a great adventure and opportunity to immerse myself in the French culture while taking a live history lesson. It was an incredible experience for a very young man.

The backstories of those that helped Dad escape are unimaginable and inspiring. These were simple farmers, shopkeepers, policemen, and doctors. They weren't soldiers. They were just your neighbors. But each of them had decided that his country and the freedom of his family and friends was best served by aiding Allied soldiers, even at the cost of his own life.

You will hear about some of these folks. In particular, those that helped Dad: Maurice, Paulin, Dr. Charlin, both Henris, and Josefa, amongst others. It was their undaunted courage in the face of evil that brought so many of the flyboys home.

INTRODUCTION

It was still dark as fifty-four B-17s spiraled upwards around radio splasher beacons to break out finally at twenty thousand feet. When the lead plane of the Ninety-Second Bomb Group fired its flares, the roaring "Heavies" began to form up. Twenty-year-old George Starks maneuvered his plane into its assigned position: low squadron, low group, flying number six in a bomber box formation—the most exposed and therefore vulnerable spot within the entire configuration. Airmen called it the "coffin corner" because, they said, "you were more likely to have your ass shot down from there than any other place."

After more than an hour, the entire wing of more than a hundred planes was flying over the narrowest part of the English Channel, the Straight of Dover. George ordered his crew to test their weapons. Thirteen heavy machine guns opened up, their recoil rippling through the plane. In the cockpit, empty brass shell casings rained down around the pilot's seat from the upper turret, clattering as they hit metal flooring. The smell of cordite permeated the air.

All positions reported back "OK" while George continued to hold close formation. Though they had trained as a crew for several months, this was their first mission together. Their average age was twenty-two.

Suddenly cloud cover began to break, and the coastline of France loomed ahead. On his four previous missions, the young pilot had encountered heavy flak over land, but on this day everything seemed unusually still. They lumbered deeper into Europe toward Augsburg, Germany, with little fire coming from below.

Which made the next event of that morning—March 16, 1944— even more startling. George never saw the Fw 190 that hit him. They were flying along when he felt a slight shudder. Later he learned the enemy fighter had dived down through the formation and pulled up under his left wing. In a near-acrobatic maneuver—which under friendlier circumstances might have been awe-inspiring—the German pilot "stood his plane on its tail and walked its stream of fire with rudders." The Fw 190 had pummeled their left wing with ammunition.

Somebody yelled, "Fire! Fire!" and mayhem broke out as ten young men realized what was happening. The first one in immediate jeopardy was the ball turret gunner. Fire spread along the plane's belly, quickly heating up the hanging plexiglass turret. Intense urgency filled his voice. "Can I come out, Captain? It's gettin' pretty hot down here."

"Yes, yes—get out!" cried George as he desperately feathered the engine. It sputtered and shut down. Flames continued to advance, rapidly melting the "skin" away from the plane's skeleton. Seeing fire leaping to the second engine on his left, George knew it was hopeless. He was carrying ten five hundred-pound bombs that would destroy other planes if they exploded, leaving him no alternative but to pull the large bomber out of formation. He screamed the final order, "Abandon ship!" into the intercom, though several of the crew were already adjusting their parachute harnesses.

As he scrambled to get out of his seat, he looked down the center of the plane. Most crewmen had already bailed out or were in the process of exiting through the hatch closest to their gunnery position. Then he spotted two crewmen hesitating at the bomb bay doors. George couldn't tell who they were since their faces now were covered with helmets and oxygen masks.

He ran up to them. As he approached, one crewman flung himself out into the roaring wind, but the other stood frozen, his arms braced against the sides of the hatch like a cat above a sink full of water. "Go! Go!" George yelled from behind, but the other young man remained motionless, staring down into contrails ripping past. Without another thought, George lunged forward. Both airmen went flying out the door into freezing air five miles up...plunging downward into a totally unknown world filled with risk and injury, death, and war.

PART I

BEGINNINGS

CHAPTER 1

RECONNECTING:
THE "SEARCH" TRIP

May 29, 1969

George Wiley Starks had written a letter to the man primarily responsible for his escape to Switzerland from occupied France during World War II, though they'd had no contact for nearly twenty-five years. People in French villages just don't move around much, he had told his wife, Betty Jo, and George mailed a letter to the only address he had: Vaux et Chantegrue, in the Doubs department, where Maurice Baverel had lived when they met at the most discouraging point of the young pilot's desperate attempt to reach neutral territory.

Within a few weeks, George heard back. Often over the years he had wished to retrace the three hundred-mile journey he had made on a broken foot, mostly walking alone, through the heavily German-occupied countryside in 1944. But after the war, life had imposed its own repressive template: attending college, starting a dental practice, caring for a severely handicapped daughter, and serving his country again—two years in Korea, part of that time in the frozen Chosin Reservoir. The circumstances of his life had been demanding, and the right moment had never come. George finally decided that if he was ever to make the journey, now was the time.

Planning his trip, he sent more letters to addresses hastily jotted down on a scrap of paper he had kept all these years in his sock drawer. Anything written during his time of evading enemy troops in France could have gotten the helpers or himself shot. What he had recorded later in England was from memory.

So this tattered paper corner, plus one letter written in Polish he had received upon his return to the states from a woman who'd hidden him that first night in a foreign land, was all that connected him with any of the brave souls across the ocean. But the thought of reuniting with even one or two of the men, women, and children who had assisted him evoked a sense of awe. He couldn't wait to see them again if—and this was a big if—he could find them. He wondered whether some would still be alive.

One day while George was mulling over flight and hotel reservations with his wife, the phone rang. Carl Langford, mayor of Orlando, Florida, had heard from common friends about George's plan to retrace his journey through France and asked if there was anything he could do to help. The two men began to formulate an idea.

Within a couple of weeks, George returned from an appointment with Mayor Langford clutching ten large packets that brought a smile to his face every time he thought about them. These packages were the first items tucked away in his suitcase the day the Starks left for Europe.

After arriving in Luxembourg, the couple drove their black rented Volkswagen to Rheims, France. Checking into a small hotel a half block from the train station, George spent a night nearly sleepless with excitement about seeing his old friend the next day.

The next morning—a lovely, clean-smelling May day—the Starkses went to greet the eleven o'clock train on which Maurice Baverel was traveling. Up and down the platform George paced, looking for what he remembered, a twenty-seven-year-old Frenchman of slight build with a headful of dark, wavy hair, whom, for the rest of his life, he would refer to as the bravest man he had ever known.

The platform cleared, and the disappointed couple returned to their hotel room, hoping Maurice had simply missed his train. Presently, a crisp rap at the door brought George to his feet. When he opened it, there stood a middle-aged man grinning from ear to ear. "What happened to your hair?" said George to the nearly bald Frenchman before him, and with that, the two men who had shared death-defying adventures when the world was at war embraced with instantly renewed camaraderie.

———

That evening, Jo sat in a small café listening to her husband and Maurice talk nearly non-stop. Maurice had taught himself some English, certainly much more than he knew when he and George first met. Even the proprietor had joined them for a while, entertaining everyone with a cartoon picture of George parachuting into France from his flaming B-17, drawn on the back of a menu.

Jo had heard the stories so many times over the years that she could name the people and places almost as well as George could. But sitting with this hero of the French Resistance, who had supplied information throughout the war to British and American intelligence agencies, seeing him in the flesh, watching the two men laughing and reminiscing, somehow brought all of it to life in ways she hardly could have imagined. Knowing she might meet people during the next few days who had saved George's life many times, and always at the risk of their own, as well as those of their families, brought fresh tears.

In those moments, Jo thought back to the first time she and George had met. She was only twelve, he was sixteen. However, she was just two years behind him in school because of the accelerated promotions common in the 1930s and '40s. He was fond of saying—and said it often—

that she was the cutest thing he had ever seen. The captain of the Suwannee High School band in Live Oak, Florida, he loved goosing her from behind with his trombone as she, a majorette, led the way.

He was eighteen when he went off to war, and she was fourteen. They weren't sweethearts yet, but she gave him a picture of herself to take with him, which he kept all through flight training and eventually brought to Podington, England. When he returned from war, they resumed their friendship, which quickly led to something more serious. And after many dates on George's motorcycle, the Green Hornet, they wed at All Saints Episcopal Church of Live Oak. The marriage would last sixty-six years.

—————

Eager to get started the next morning, George, Jo, and Maurice squeezed into the Volkswagen. Maurice drove, George up front beside him, Betty Jo sandwiched between everybody's luggage in the back seat. They traveled southeast, toward the place where the adventure had begun for George and his crew just north of Vitry-le-François on March 16, 1944. Here, in the village of Bronne, in the region of Champagne-Ardenne, George's plane had crashed. Later in 1944, American infantrymen would endure the coldest winter of the twentieth century fighting the German offensive in the Ardennes that came to be known as the Battle of the Bulge.

But on this day, the sun glistened. And George and Maurice relished one another's company, riding carefree through the French countryside. When they arrived at the village, George's anticipation grew, hoping against all odds they could somehow locate where his B-17 had come down.

Driving slowly through the narrow country lanes, Maurice spotted a couple of locals walking along. Rolling down the window, he hailed them to the car and abruptly inquired if they knew where a B-17 had crashed anywhere nearby in March 1944.

Jo wondered how anyone could ask such a question, since they had been shot down over a quarter of a century earlier. Who in the world could possibly know exactly where their plane had crashed? George himself was mildly amused at Maurice's question—until, that is, one of the men said, "Mais oui, mais oui," and offered to take them to the spot, in a field on his father's farm.

The former pilot felt a sudden rush. Could it possibly be this simple? That they would just drive into France and be led to the spot where his plane had ended up? The Frenchman motioned them to follow, and soon they arrived at a large, serenely beautiful field with a long row of trees running the length of one side.

They drove the VW nearly to the tree line, then got out and walked the rest of the way. As they approached a large depression in the ground, now overgrown with grass, their eager guide pointed to the area, explaining to Maurice what had happened on March 16, 1944, when he witnessed the B-17 plummeting to earth.

His father had been plowing close by when exploding sounds from crashing metal caused both workhorses to bolt, wrenching free and tearing off across the field. About the same time, he saw at a distance two parachutists land, only to be immediately apprehended by German soldiers. George realized that they had to have been his navigator, Ted Badder, and bombardier, Irv Baum, who had dropped fairly close to one another.

When George reached the large sunken area, he could hardly fathom he was standing on the precise spot where his plane had come down. They all poked around through twenty-five years of debris. Soon, however, the ground began yielding up silent markers of the catastrophic event: handfuls of unfired shells.

As they were digging around, the farmer's enthusiasm began to visibly mount. He excitedly motioned for all of them to follow him back to his cottage. There, Marius Tosquin hastened inside to retrieve something that he had displayed on the mantle above his fireplace for twenty-five years. He returned with an object he obviously considered a treasure, and as soon as George saw what it was, he knew the whole trip to France had been worth it—even if this was the only thing he retrieved.

George extended his hands to receive the gift, and in the next moment he was holding a pair of thick, sheepskin-lined, brown leather long gloves with the index finger and thumb separated from the remaining mitt—the unmistakable gloves of a gunner from a B-17—pointer finger and thumb separated so the gunner could pull the trigger of his weapon, fleece-lined to protect his hands and arms from the stinging cold of twenty-eight thousand feet. George knew his tail gunner, Dick Morse, had thrown down a pair just like that in the rear section of his plane seconds before he bailed out.

Still it was incredible that George had found this farmer. Tosquin explained that as soon as the fires from the wreckage had died down that morning, he had combed through the site, finding the gloves, unharmed, in the tail section, which had broken off from the fuselage, almost intact. He had found also a strut, ammo cans, a porthole, and an oxygen tank, which they had stored in their barn all these years. He added there were also some pictures. George asked to see them.

They followed Tosquin inside the cottage, where the Frenchman produced three small photographs, and sure enough, there were Bob Williams, Don Edgerly, and Bill Wyatt, his radio operator, engineer, and ball turret gunner—head shots taken in civilian clothes before the young men had left England to be used for identification purposes in case they were shot down. These three men had been hidden for a few days after they first came down in Vavray-le-Grand by the Lambert family, relatives of Tosquin. While there, these pictures had been duplicated in the village before they began trying to make their way to Switzerland.

The middle-aged farmer stood grinning, obviously pleased to be able to provide such choice trophies for the former American bomber pilot. Maurice stood there, joyous at having led his friend to just the right spot, as he had done many times in helping George cross the border into Switzerland. George stood there, enraptured at finding this place at all, not to mention the gloves and photographs, after twenty-five years. And Jo—well, Jo just stood there trying to keep from crying again.

———

After loading up these "souvenirs," the trio readied themselves for their journey into Vitry-en-Perthois. From this point forward, each turn of the road, each vista, each house seemed to bring back some memory with a vividness George had not experienced since returning home to Florida after the war.

As George rode along, hoping that he would find more of the people who had helped him in his desperation—with a twenty-millimeter shell fragment embedded in his calf and a tarsal fracture in his right foot, hungry, scared, alone, with no idea where he was or whom he could trust, wondering what had happened to his crew, Krauts everywhere combing the countryside—he began to think back to where it all had started: his junior year in high school, 1940, in the National Guard Unit of Live Oak, Florida.

CHAPTER 2

BEGINNING AT SIXTEEN

In Live Oak—population 3,427 according to the 1940 census—the Guard met every Wednesday night. The group served its official purposes with the added bonus of a place to hang out with other young guys. George, only sixteen at the time, had talked a bunch of his buddies into joining. In a small town where everybody knew everybody else, they all knew he wasn't old enough.

But even at sixteen, he was so personable and well-liked, they overlooked his age. Those two traits, along with the boyish looks that lasted long into his adult life, served him well many times—as they did four years later when the Gestapo mistook him for *under* sixteen, their cut-off age for requiring identification papers.

Once the Guard was federalized for the war effort that was cranking up before Pearl Harbor, the local office told him he would have to be discharged because of his age. Immediately upon graduating from high school, however, George found out the Army Aviation Cadet Program was allowing entrance to those who didn't meet the usual requirement of two years of college if they scored high enough on the written and physical tests. So as soon as he graduated from Suwannee High in 1941, he hitchhiked to Orlando to take the tests and was one of the five applicants out of fifty who passed, though he only squeaked through on the physical part.

It wasn't that he lacked health or ability. George stood six feet tall but weighed a meager 124 pounds. A chief master sergeant in charge of physical exams for hundreds of applicants, noting his outstanding written score, told him to go eat a dozen bananas and milkshakes and come back. Later that day, George climbed back on the scales at the noisy, crowded recruiting center and topped out at 126, still two pounds shy of the required 128 pounds for his height. The sergeant shook his head and said, "Oh, hell, just go on."

And with that, George Wiley Starks, the band captain from Suwannee High School, Live Oak, Florida, began a journey, young by anybody's standards, toward becoming the pilot of a B-17, the heavy bomber known as the Flying Fortress, in the mighty Eighth Air Force. He'd be responsible for an aircraft that cost a staggering $238,329 to build and carried up to seventeen thousand pounds of high explosive and incendiary bombs, plus thirteen .50 caliber machine guns, and a crew of nine men. All because of a few bananas and milkshakes and a busy, exasperated sergeant who pushed him over the qualifying line.

━━━━

Entering cadets went to the Berryhill U.S. Army Air Corp classification center at Nashville for evaluation, which included physical and psychological tests, plus hand-eye coordination exams. George qualified for three positions—pilot, navigator, and bombardier. He chose to be a pilot, something he'd always wanted to do. In fact, he had taken a couple of flying lessons when he had any extra money.

In September 1942, he was sent to Maxwell Field in Montgomery, Alabama, for pre-flight school. Like most of his basic training, it had its memorable moments, usually more pleasant in hindsight, like Saturday morning PT, which involved running seven to nine miles around the field, double-time. The guys called it the Burma Road, and after they finished they were free to leave the post from one o'clock on Saturday afternoon until nine o'clock on Sunday night. Most, however, were so tired after PT they just remained on base.

When he finished at Maxwell, George left for Union City, Tennessee, to begin primary flight school. Pilot training took place in five stages of nine weeks each. It wasn't long before George, in a leather helmet and goggles, was flying in the open cockpit of a PT-17.

On June 30, 1943, nineteen-year-old George Starks received his wings and shiny gold bars and headed for Lockbourne Army Airfield (now Rickenbacker International Airport) in Columbus, Ohio, for B-17 training. Afterwards, he received three months of combat training at Pyote Army Air Field, located in the middle of nowhere, Texas.[1] His group, one of twenty-six, was slated to replenish an existing group that had sustained heavy losses. From there the group traveled to Grand Island, Nebraska, where George, along with his newly assigned crew, was given a brand new B-17G.

These boys, from all over the United States, represented a wide range of backgrounds, interests, and dreams. Their average age of twenty-two made the waist gunner, Wallace "Wally" Trinder, an "old man at twenty-seven, and the rest of them called him 'Pops.'" But for George, this was now his crew and his plane, and he was proud of both.

After ten months of training, they were ready to fly across the North Atlantic Route to England and the war, not knowing what lay ahead but filled with the enthusiasm of youth. Buzzing the housetops of waist gunner Arden "Andy" Brenden's hometown of Starbuck, Minnesota, they made their way to Goose Bay, Labrador.[2] It was the first time the boy pilot from Florida had ever seen that much snow or had tried ice skating.

––––––––

The morning of takeoff in mid-January 1944 was cold and foggy at Goose Bay, and the snowy embankments on both sides of the runway were coated with ice. A "Follow Me" jeep led planes away from hangars down the paved corridors from which they attempted to get airborne, having to spiral up to clear the nearby mountains. George's plane was one of only two that were able to get off that morning.

As they crossed the North Atlantic, the pilot, co-pilot, navigator, and radio operator manned their respective positions, watching dials, checking instruments. The other crewmen—bombardier, both waist gunners, ball turret gunner, tail gunner, and engineer—just focused on keeping warm in the belly of the plane for the 2,500-mile flight to England. Traveling at about 287 miles per hour through the severest weather conditions any of them had ever flown in, their aircraft fully loaded with spare parts and materiel on one side and balanced by four hundred gallons of fuel on the other, the crew expected the journey to take nine hours.

And it should have. Except that a few hours into the flight, George asked his co-pilot, Warren Wilson, to take the controls while he rested. Having flown only on instruments since takeoff and exhausted by the schedule of the past few months, George lay back in his seat, propping his feet up on the rudder bars. When he awakened a half-hour later, he glanced at the magnetic compass and bolted forward. "We're headed into the middle of the Atlantic!" he yelled after seeing the needle pointing due south.

At crew reunions decades afterwards, memories differed as to how the plane got off course. However it happened, the roaring B-17 was redirected toward England, though low fuel made a premature landing necessary. Fortunately, the coast of Ireland loomed ahead. "Darkie, Darkie" (the emergency call sign to radio operators standing by in England to assist), "this is EndWays-Yoke, this is EndWays-Yoke," the crew's emergency code name. Almost immediately, the bomber was re-routed to Knutt's Corner on the Emerald Isle. When they descended out of the thick clouds, the navigator negotiated one turn and lined them up directly with the runway. After flying who-knows-how-many miles, George landed them safely in the heavy fog and rain.

CHAPTER 3

ONLY ONE JUMP...EVER

For more than three years, the United States military had been flying men and equipment to England almost daily. The trip usually ended with a train ride to their destination base. George Starks and his crew went by boat from Ireland to England, then by troop train to Podington, about seventy-five miles north of London.[1]

Once there, the officers were grouped twelve to fifteen men per Quonset hut and participated in practice flights before beginning actual missions. Stories circulating among the pilots gave each man much to ponder. At the time, twenty-five bombing missions were required before you could return home. Later the requirement was raised to thirty, then thirty-five, as fighter protection increased. But in early 1944, flying unescorted, only about one out of every ten men made it to his twenty-five missions. George listened, wondering, as they all did, if he would be the lucky one out of ten.

Crews practiced in an area north of the base known as the Wash, the largest shallow bay of the North Sea, which jutted deep into England's eastern coastline. Over this enormous remote estuary, B-17s and other planes could practice in relative safety, gaining experience with the unpredictable weather conditions of the Channel and sea.[2]

"Relative" safety was, well, relative. On one of George's practice runs, his group began taking heavy flak. Immediately radio communication ramped up, only to discover it was coming from ground forces who mistook them for enemy aircraft. George was reminded of the time he had been summoned out onto the runway back at Lockbourne Army Air Base to complete a couple of hours remaining in one of his training categories. Dressed in flight gear and about to board a B-17 to participate as a crew member, he was stopped by a sergeant who came running out from the hangar and told him they had miscalculated—he didn't need any more hours. The plane took off without him. Returning three hours later, the plane burst into flames on its approach, killing the entire crew.

Near misses like this one and the one over the Wash began to mount up. After the war, George often said he had an angel watching over him the entire time. No friend or family member who knew his whole story ever disagreed.

━━━━

For young men away from their hometown, many for the first time, London nightlife made a lasting impression. George joined a private establishment called the Studio Club, where jazz bands and singers serenaded young Yanks on weekend passes late into the evening. Pubs stayed open most of the night, offering food, beer, and pleasant hours away from war and bombing missions. But the reason they were so many thousands of miles from home was always in the back of their minds.

George had traveled into the metropolis a couple of times since his arrival in mid-January. On one weekend trip in early March 1944, he went with his co-pilot, Warren Wilson, whom the crew called "Willy." They heard a drop-dead gorgeous blonde who sang "I'll Be Seeing You," and everyone there swooned into his mug. As the singer stopped several times at the table of the handsome and boyish bomber pilot, George grinned from ear to ear.

On this evening, however, Betty Jo, the pretty little majorette back home, kept coming to mind. She was sweet sixteen now, and the new drum major at their high school back in Live Oak. For a second, the staccato sounds of marching band music overcame the smoky strains of the London jazz group. But in the next moment, the singer with the low, sultry voice swished by his table once more and he was pulled back into reality—a twenty-year-old senior pilot flying one of the finest airplanes ever built, on intense bombing missions meant to bring victory to the United States of America and its allies in a world war. Drinking down the last of his beer, he and Willy headed back to Hotel Piccadilly.

———

The end of February 1944 saw American bombers launching what was known as Big Week, a period of sustained bombing over Regensburg, Augsburg, and Forth, all significant areas of factories, munitions depots, and artillery banks. By the end of February, 226 bombers had been lost during these engagements. While 1944 eventually became the tipping point of the war, the first six months remained tenuous. D-Day was still only a plan on the generals' drawing boards.

During each afternoon at RAF Podington, a base officially made available on April 18, 1942, to the United States Army Air Forces Eighth Air Force, the busiest place on the air station became the bulletin board where the next day's assignments were posted. George Wiley Starks, who had just checked out of the infirmary after a severe ear infection, looked over the roster and saw that his crew was to participate in the mission leaving at daybreak the following morning, March 16, 1944. It would be their first mission together as a crew.

At mess that evening, he learned that Willy, his co-pilot, had accidentally shot himself in the left hand while cleaning his pistol. His replacement would be Lieutenant Dale Beery, flying with the crew for the first time. Although George had participated in four bombing missions since he arrived in Podington, he had flown only as co-pilot. Tomorrow would be different—he would be the pilot. Sleep that night came sporadically.

———

About four o'clock the next morning, the Charge of Quarters on duty jostled through the huts, waving a flashlight, calling out an abrupt wake-up signal. Trucks began shuttling the crews into the mess hall for a breakfast of fresh eggs and powdered milk. As soon as the crews gulped this down, they headed for the main briefing session. It was here George met his new co-pilot—a man whose life would intersect with his for only about six hours—but those six hours would forever change the life of each man.

The entire group watched as briefing officers pulled the curtain down, revealing a large board with a map. They outlined the mission to Augsburg, located between Stuttgart and Munich. Each squadron was given information about its target. George's squadron would be bombing the Dornier aircraft manufacturing plant at Oberpfaffenhofen, an important target because of its innovative fighter designs and production.

After the briefing, crews filed out to the trucks waiting to take them to their B-17s. The young pilot began pulling on his flight suit, then a jacket and pants, something akin to wearing a dark-green heated blanket that plugged into the plane's electrical system.

It was still black and cold when all the crewmen positioned themselves inside the bomber. The tail gunner as usual entered through a separate hatch at the back of the aircraft, the other four gunners through the main side door. The pilot, co-pilot, engineer, navigator, and bombardier all entered through the nose hatch, some swinging up feet first. Everyone began checking his controls and equipment in his own space, acutely aware they soon would be flying over Germany, meeting up with fighters, ground fire, or probably both.

But for the moment, getting airborne held its own challenges. Forming up could take as long as an hour, sometimes an hour and a half. With hundreds of aircraft taking off at thirty-second intervals, the skies filled quickly with the roar of more than a thousand engines, at first seeming more like laboring beasts than airworthy craft, spiraling slowly upward until each was in position, waiting like fidgeting school children for the last student to fall in line. It was a dangerous part of flying that most pilots dreaded.

Finally, the formation was complete and several thousand tons of bombs and ammunition turned toward the coast of Europe as dawn began to break through the clouds. For the boys of B-17 number 42-31022, which pulled into its assigned position—low squadron, low group flying the number six position, known as "coffin corner" because of its exposure, a position usually given to the new, lower-ranking replacements—it would be a very long day.

———

As bombers from the Ninety-Second Bomb Group crossed the Channel and moved into France, morning duskiness gave way to mostly clear skies with spotted cumulus clouds. Everything seemed to be going smoothly. So far they had been met with little or no resistance.

But as the large group of unescorted "Heavies" rumbled deeper into France, the first group of Fw 190s spotted the bombers. These German fighters, nicknamed *Würger*, or "butcher birds," flew at speeds of nearly four hundred miles per hour and had splendid maneuverability. They were a pilot's airplane, and the German airmen learned quickly the vulnerable spots within the B-17 formations.

Three German pilots claimed hits that morning: Major Heinz Huppertz at 10:40 a.m., Lieutenant Karlheinz Elsner at 10:41 a.m., and

Lieutenant Christoph Decius at 10:44 a.m. Judging from the sheer skill of the maneuvers witnessed by the ball turret gunner and others, it was probably Huppertz who actually shot out the number one engine. He was one of Germany's premier flying aces, and before his death at twenty-five shortly after D-Day, he had registered over sixty shoot-downs, many on the Eastern Front.

Regardless of who it was in the Fw 190, George never saw the fighter coming in. Approaching from above, then splitting and diving down, it came up underneath the formation with lightning speed, placing a direct hit underneath George's left wing, just beside number one engine, which almost immediately began to sputter. It caught fire and shut down completely. From this point, everything was a blur.

Staying in formation for several more seconds, George heard his ball turret gunner yelling into the intercom for permission to leave his position. Flames were already lapping against the turret making it impossible to stay there. Meanwhile, the pilot of the squadron's lead plane, looking back and seeing the number-six plane's left wing blazing, told his crew he was going to count to ten, and if they didn't move out of formation by then, he was going to shoot off the tail section.

About that time, George realized he had no other option but to pull out of formation lest an explosion jeopardize the other planes. He rang the emergency bell and called the crew on intercom to abandon ship. Each man began a frantic scramble to the closest hatch. All the gunners flew with their harnesses on and their parachutes close by on the floor. The pilot, co-pilot, engineer, navigator, and bombardier also wore harnesses, their parachutes tucked beneath their seats.

On his way out of the cockpit, the co-pilot had reached under George's seat, pulled his parachute out, and thrown it on his lap. George unbuckled his seat belt and began making his way toward the back of the plane, all the time fumbling to get his parachute hooked into place. Looking down through the body of the plane, he could see only two crew members left.

He ran up to them not knowing for sure who they were, since their faces were covered with equipment. One of them had eyes as big as saucers. The three stood there staring at each other for a split second. Then one bailed out the door. The plane began to lurch, and the pilot pushed forward into the back of the man in front of him. They both tumbled out into minus-thirty-three-degree air. It was the one and only jump George would make in his entire life.

PART II

THE CREW AND
FIRST DAYS DOWN

CHAPTER 4

A WHISTLE SIGNAL: GEORGE STARKS, PILOT

The rest of the crew had opened high right after bailing out. But I decided to free fall. I wasn't wearing my fur-lined flight suit on this mission but had elected to use a thinner suit that heated from the plane's electrical system. I knew, however, I couldn't survive the cold at that altitude for long.

Only seconds after I left the plane—it looked near enough to touch—the left wing blew off and the bomber went into a flat spin and crashed far below, near the French hamlet of Bronne. I was still free falling and found that if I kept my arms and legs crossed, I didn't spin so badly and fell feet first. Terminal velocity for the human body is about 130 miles per hour, so I was going down rather rapidly.

I never did see any of the crew in their chutes—they had all opened high. Baum told me after the war that two German fighters made passes at him on the way down, and he was afraid they were going to shoot, but a P-47 came and chased them off. Bob Williams had the *same experience. A mix of four to six Me 109s and Fw 190s buzzed him, and again an American fighter (P-51) ran them off and then circled him down to the ground.*

Anyway, I was free falling and saw the tops of some lower cumulus beneath me. I figured those tops were about six thousand feet and decided to open when I got there. Just before going into the clouds, I pulled the ripcord and chuted down through them.

When I broke out of the bottom of the overcast at two to three thousand feet, I saw I was falling directly toward some large trees, so I pulled on the risers to steer clear. One of the crew, I later learned, was injured pretty badly when he hit, but I missed the trees and landed hard, not realizing at the time I suffered a hairline fracture in my right foot, nor that I had a 20mm fragment in my thigh—adrenaline, I guess.

Right after I hit and scooped up the chute, I saw a P-47 coming my way, very low. He was probably returning from a mission and flying low for home when he saw my chute. At any rate, he banked back around and slowed with his gear and flaps down to look at the prospects of landing in the large pasture nearby. They would do that, you know. If they could land, they would piggy-back you out of there—sitting on your lap to fly the plane and scoot you both home.

He made a second low pass over the field with the engine throttled back to a low grumble. But it was too hilly. He looked at me through his plexiglass bubble canopy, shook his head, waggled his wings, and flew on.

So there I was, lost in occupied territory, wondering what to do next and having no idea that a three-hundred-kilometer escape attempt, on foot, still lay ahead. I got rid of the parachute, moved closer to a road nearby, and hid for a while in some small trees with underbrush, waiting to see what would happen next.[1]

═══════

The peaceful quiet of a French countryside morning enveloped the downed pilot and would have been a welcome balm if George hadn't soon heard dry foliage rustling nearby. Carefully peering through the brush, he could make out several German soldiers, rifles ready, not more than thirty feet away, obviously searching for him or others they had spotted coming down. They had stopped their truck not far from where a group of Frenchmen were working on the road, slightly above where George had buried himself in the leaves.

He held perfectly still for what seemed an eternity. Finally, the soldiers continued across the field and disappeared over a small hill. George stayed hunkered down in the brush, planning to remain there until after dark. But about mid-afternoon, one of the Frenchmen who was working on the roadway when the Germans had searched earlier came walking slowly into the woods, making a signal with a whistle. George waited until he was certain the man was alone and then came out of hiding. At this point, he wasn't sure what else could be done.

After emerging from his hiding place, George noticed the man was carrying a small bottle of wine with some bread and cigarettes. The man spoke no English but pointed to himself, saying "Paulin Crete," obviously a quick introduction, and then indicated on his watch he would return after dark, about eight o'clock. There was nothing to do except climb back into the brush and sip wine, hoping his new "friend" could be trusted.

Close to eight o'clock, Crete returned alone. He motioned George to follow him through the woods to a small town north of Vitry-le-François called Vitry-en-Perthois. They passed through narrow streets into an alleyway accessed behind a low fence. Reaching a small house, the helper stopped and tapped quietly on the door. A lady answered and motioned them quickly in. She lived with her eight-year-old daughter and, through sign language and broken phrases, indicated she was Polish and that her husband was a prisoner of war in Germany. Her name was Josefa Wilczynska, and her daughter was Marie Claire.

Through the evening, other neighbors came bringing pieces of civilian clothes. George took off his uniform but kept his woolen long-handles and wool army socks because the season remained cold. A coarse grey work shirt and dark pants made up the primary pieces—the shirt fit well enough, but the pants were too short and too large in the waist, so George rolled the extra fabric over a rope and cinched it tight. He scuffed his low-quarter shoes with a rock, rubbing away their shiny military finish.

Because of the cold he kept his flight jacket but stripped off the badges and insignia. On top of all this, the helpers placed a thin trench coat buttoned to the top to conceal everything. Someone brought a small, canvas haversack with a bottle of wine, black bread, and cheese. George also stuffed in some of the survival items issued before the flight: 2,000 francs, water purification pills, concentrated food bars, a silk road map,[2] and a dime-sized compass. He handed over his Colt .45 to the mayor of the village, who had joined the group. George didn't want to chance being caught with a gun. Germans usually shot anyone found carrying a weapon.

Before Madame Wilczynska led George to a small cot on the first floor where he could spend the night, the helpers added one final touch— a black beret. Since Frenchmen generally wore their hair long, a GI haircut would be a give-away. They warned him against walking through the city of Vitry-le-Françoise—too many Germans. He was to cut across country due south, joining the main road beyond that town and heading southwest toward Saint-Dizier.

George fell asleep clutching the haversack, buoyed by the kindness of these first few French "helpers" he had met, especially the brave Polish woman, living alone with her child, who might never see her husband again. The next morning, he woke early and left, heading south toward Switzerland.

———

I walked along the road hoping I looked French. Too many German trucks rumbled past—close enough to touch. Staff cars, too…tanks that shook the road…Germans on grey motorcycles with sidecars…foot soldiers carrying packs and Mauser rifles. … I tried to pay them no mind and kept walking.

Food items from the haversack helped me stave off hunger, and I drank from public wells in the villages as I went along. But for the most part I just kept moving…not many rest stops and always avoiding encounters with people as best I could.

I walked too far that day: nearly forty kilometers. In a hurry, I guess. Anyway, I burned a bad blister on my foot somewhere before I got to Saint-Dizier. I skirted the town and kept walking to put Saint-Dizier's concentration of Germans behind me. Later I learned Badder and Baum, picked up that first day, had been apprehended by gendarmes who turned them over to Germans for a reward. My two crewmen were being held at a German installation with an air field—one I actually passed as I walked around the outskirts.

Night was coming on and I needed a place to stop. A few kilometers south of Saint-Dizier, I came to a railroad crossing—near Bienville, maybe. A small, neat two-story stucco house stood there alone beside the train tracks—possibly the railroad crossing guard's house.

My foot and leg were burning. I decided to chance it. Going up to the front door, I knocked and recited my lines in pigeon French I'd learned the night before: "Je suis pilote américain. Parachute en France. Partais à Suisse."

The French railroad guard was about my age, lived alone, accepted my story, and took me in. I stayed there two nights, resting and letting my foot heal somewhat. He removed the bits of shrapnel from my thigh and washed and bandaged my blistered foot. It had swelled up, beyond what seemed likely—the first time I realized I might have broken something parachuting down.

When I left, he also warned me to stay out of large towns, so I chose country lanes that paralleled the highway as best I could. Except for my foot, the walking was actually fairly easy with rolling countryside. The mountains were to come later.[3]

CHAPTER 5

BETRAYED BY THE GENDARMES: TED BADDER, NAVIGATOR

Ted Badder was the only "Yank" in his family. Not because his relatives were all Southerners and he was from the North, but because they were all from Great Britain. He was the only one in his family, including parents and siblings, to have been born in the United States. His father, originally from Bristol, and his mother, from Liverpool, had moved to the United States after listening to her brothers, who had migrated there after the First World War. Ted's grandparents still lived in Cardiff, Wales, and he had traveled there a few times with his parents, once making the transatlantic passage on the *Queen Mary*. Returning to Britain in 1943 seemed more like going back home than going to war.

Ted's father had served in the British army for more than thirty-five years, fighting in the Boer Wars and in Egypt. The sterling silver pocket watch with its engraved inscription—CS Badder, 3rd Royal Guards Regiment—presented to the color sergeant major when he retired, remains a prized family heirloom today.

Ted had grown up hearing war stories, not just from his father but from his mother as well. During those years of British imperialism, soldiers were allowed to travel with their families. Ted's mother had as much knowledge of places and things like Wadi Halfa, camels, and "Fuzzy Wuzzies" as his father did, the latter referring to the brave Hadendoa warriors the British fought in the Sudan and who were eulogized later in poems by Rudyard Kipling. If ever a young man deemed fighting alongside England appropriate, it was Ted Badder.

In 1940, after graduating from high school, Ted took a job in New York City working as a "runner" for an insurance company. Since his family lived in Woodridge, about a hundred miles from the city, his weekly salary of fifty-five dollars was consumed by tolls, train fares, and bus tickets, and he gave some of each paycheck to his parents. After these expenses, he netted about fifteen dollars a week.

One day on the way home from work, he unexpectedly ran into a friend from high school dressed in an army uniform. As they talked, Ted found out that if a young man joined the army, his parents received compensation as well if they were partially dependent on his support. He immediately went to the recruiting office and began the process of enlisting. The recruiter suggested the Air Corps, but when he learned that Badder had never been in an airplane, he advised the young man simply to enlist and go into deskwork.

Ted could type sixty words per minute, a skill so prized by the captain to whom he was assigned at Barksdale Field near Shreveport, Louisiana, that he kept Ted's desk next to his own in the hangar where they kept the records of cadets learning to fly. Every day, the captain encouraged the young private to join him as a passenger when he went up to check out a plane, but Badder always found an excuse.

One day the captain threw a parachute into Ted's lap, announcing, "Today is the day." In a few moments, Ted was up in the air in an AT-6 Texan looking down at Shreveport and the Red River. To his surprise, he enjoyed the experience—in fact, he enjoyed it immensely. After that, he went up nearly every time the captain went, and when the Army Air Corps lowered its requirements for the Flying Sergeant program from two years of college to just a high school diploma, Ted found himself in Americus, Georgia, learning to fly a PT-17 biplane painted bright yellow and blue.

━━━━━━

Badder had flown about twelve hours or so when he went up for his first solo. He had flown around for a while and was now looking over the side of the Stearman's open cockpit to locate the landing strip. Suddenly he realized he had gone too far and was coming in too fast over the trees. He looked down to see his flight instructor and several others furiously waving their arms trying to direct him in.

Once he was down, his instructor said, "Ted, you're a nice guy, but you're kinda slow up there." With that, Badder washed out of pilot school, but he made it into navigation school in Monroe, Louisiana. For the next nine months, he almost always had a small octant in his hands, practicing shooting the stars and sun. He usually flew with three others in the second-row seats of a Beechcraft AT-7, the plane used most often to train navigators in World War I.

Just as in days of old, when Britannia ruled the waves and much of military life depended on celestial navigation, a good navigator was worth his weight in gold. Maybe navigational know-how was in Badder's English genes, but whatever the reason, he found his talent and his passion, delving into his studies with zeal. He would be able to recall nearly all twenty-six navigational stars primarily used in the Northern Hemisphere to the end of his life.

━━━━━━

Once he arrived in Pyote, Texas, Badder met his other crew members, including his pilot, George Starks. All ten young men hit it off and often did things together on weekends, not that there was that much to do in Pyote. But there was one place they all enjoyed going—Tubb's Dance Hall.

On Saturday evenings, nearly everyone from the base and the surrounding countryside ended up here—a large barn-like structure with a band, wooden picnic tables, and a dance floor. One night, as a pretty young girl danced near the crew's table, Bill Wyatt, the ball turret gunner, came over and placed his hand on Badder's shoulder. "Hey, Lieutenant, why don't you go dance with her?"

Badder hesitated, but before he knew it, Wyatt had grabbed her around the waist and danced her right over to Ted. After a whirlwind romance—not uncommon among servicemen about to ship out—the navigator and Faye were married a few days later by the base chaplain. Starks was his best man, and Faye's mother allowed them to use her Lincoln Zephyr for their honeymoon. Ted wondered why the back end of the car pitched down, until he discovered his new mother-in-law ran moonshine throughout that part of Texas.

———

Not long after Badder's wedding, the crew learned they were assigned a brand new B-17G, and they left for Ellis, Kansas, to pick it up. The landscape there was absolutely flat, and they began ferrying it from Kansas to Goose Bay, Labrador. Starks, who had never seen Niagara Falls, wanted to fly over it. After they passed the falls, the only thing Badder had to navigate by was a long, straight railroad.

The country continued to get progressively more barren, until finally there was just snow below and the railroad tracks. Arriving at Goose Bay, Badder could see only one or two blacktop roads—everything else was solid white. When they finally landed on the airstrip, the snow was piled up on both sides well over the top of the plane. Starks called on the radio that he wasn't going to budge until they dispatched a jeep out to guide them on in.

Once the crew left Goose Bay, Badder saw whitecaps in every direction as they crossed the stormy North Atlantic. And that was all that could be seen until they were over a small inlet on the map called Donegal Bay, marked by a lighthouse. Ted, his English navigational heritage on display, was only five miles south of it when they broke through the heavily overcast skies off the coast of Ireland, having covered 2,200 miles in twelve hours.

———

When they reported in Ireland, their new plane was assigned to an older, more experienced crew. Each of the young men was disappointed and almost always referred to the incident in later years with the statement, "They took our plane away from us." The new B-17G they had flown across the Atlantic had updated equipment and was reinforced with more metal plates than previous models.

Their disappointment was short-lived, however. Once they arrived in Podington, they began enjoying the sights and sounds of England, including several visits into London, taking in the popular tourist attractions like Madame Tussaud's and St. Paul's Cathedral.

But they were reminded of why they were in England by participating as substitutes with other crews in a handful of missions. When they were listed on the board for a mission into Germany on March 16, 1944, they were excited to be together for the first time, and Badder entered the B-17 assigned to them around five o'clock in the morning, while it was still pitch dark.

———

Ted Badder, Navigator

Forming up in the dark always bothered me a little. We took off into the east, but there was no light. You had hundreds of planes trying to find their leaders who were shooting off flares. As we started across the Channel and on into France, I could see out at what looked like hun-

dreds of B-17s stretching in all directions. We began cutting south because the factories we were going to were on the south side of Germany.

Everything was going fine. I'm looking out my window, and suddenly commotion broke out in the plane. Somebody says we've been hit…the next thing I know, Baum slaps me on the shoulder and yells, "Get out! Get out!" He was already trying frantically to hook his parachute onto his chest and in the rush, accidentally kicked my chute up underneath the pilot and co-pilot's seats. I scrambled for it and got to the hatch door. I really didn't want to go out…but I had no choice. I dove out with a terrible swishing of air.… I counted to three and pulled my cord. By this time the formation had gone past and there was stillness in the air.

On my way down, several Me 190s went by me—one guy actually waved to me. I kept looking down, but I couldn't see ground. When I finally broke through the clouds, I could see lots of farmland below. I tugged at the cords, trying to avoid any trees and finally hit down. The farmer had just plowed, and I sank into soft dirt. I looked down the field and saw Baum dragging his chute. We ran toward each other, and the next thing I know, we were surrounded by gendarmes. They put handcuffs on us and signaled the Germans.

When we got to town some French women brought a little soup, but they wound up putting us in a two-seat outhouse, padlocking the door. We spent the night there, and the next day we were turned over to German soldiers who took us to Frankfurt.[1]

CHAPTER 6

"ARE YOU HEBREW?": IRV BAUM, BOMBARDIER

B orn on September 11—seventy-eight years before that date became infamous—Irving Baum had lived in Monticello, New York. Most people referred to the surrounding Catskill Mountains as the "Jewish Alps" because so many Jewish families vacationed there during the summer months. Monticello itself was 99 percent Jewish, or so its residents claimed. Irv's grandfather, an Orthodox Jew who had migrated to America in the 1800s from Austria, lived with his family, and the Baums kept that side of the house kosher for his sake. Growing up in this ethnic enclave, Irv had never experienced any direct anti-Semitism.

In the 1930s, rumors of growing unrest in Europe were making their way across the Atlantic. Most Americans believed the reports of anti-Semitism were exaggerated, if there was any truth to them at all. American Jews, however, took the stories more seriously. Newspapers like the *Forward* continued to publish worrisome reports of Jews fleeing from growing tensions and persecution.

So Irv already had given some thought to how the stories of European anti-Semitism might affect his own future, but for the most part he regarded events from the point of view of any young American male who would be affected if his country went to war. In particular, Irv listened to his father's conversations with the mailman, who told stories from World War I of "mud rats" in trench warfare, and he determined that if he had to go to war, he would join one of the services well above ground level. When he came home from a Sunday matinee on December 7, 1941, and heard about Pearl Harbor, he knew that he would try to go into the service as an aviation cadet.

Enlisting in September 1942, Baum was sent first to Camp Upton, Long Island, then to Miami, and finally to Nashville, where he officially became a participant in the war effort, well above *terra firma*. By the time he reached Pyote, Texas, he had qualified for pilot and navigator but was assigned to a B-17 crew as a bombardier.

The ten men of this crew were young even by 1943 standards—Irv and George were both nineteen, and the others averaged twenty-two. They all hit it off, studying, flying, and spending their weekends together, and they all attended Ted Badder's impromptu wedding.

By the time of their stormy North Atlantic crossing, the crew's camaraderie was deep. The possibility of being shot down did not impress itself on them until they reached Podington. When they began learning about the devastating losses being sustained throughout the bomber groups in late 1943 and early '44, Irv realized that war "up in the air" would be no safer than war "down on the ground."

━━━━━

The Eighth Air Force suffered more casualties in World War II in Europe than the U.S. Marines did in the Pacific. These losses peaked in the second half of 1943 when bombing raids on the German aircraft industry took B-17s over enemy-occupied territory with few fighter escorts. The Schweinfurt-Regensburg Raid in August 1943 cost the

USAAF sixty B-17s, and 552 men were killed or taken prisoner. A similar mission on October 14, 1943, became known as "Black Thursday." Seventy-seven of the mission's 291 aircraft were lost, nearly one-third of the aircraft launched.

By the spring of 1944, it was recognized that bombing missions needed a fighter escort all the way into Germany, but a fully ramped-up P-51 Mustang program, with a new Rolls-Royce engine, was just beginning to take shape. Up to this point, the Allies had used the Thunderbolt, a P-47 without sufficient range to protect bomber formations throughout their missions. German fighter planes would hold back until the short-range Allied fighters turned back to England.

During "Big Week," February 20–25, 1944, the Allies launched a series of attacks on aircraft plants and airfields deep inside Germany. More than a thousand bombers were dispatched, and the Eighth Air Force lost ninety-seven B-17s and forty B-24s, with many more damaged beyond repair.

Reporting for duty in Podington in mid-January 1944, Starks's crew arrived in the middle of all this activity, and their mission of March 16, 1944, was scheduled just before a continuous fighter escort became the rule for most bombing missions. In the rush that morning to get to his plane on time, Baum left his parachute pack in the mess hall. Fortunately, it was found by a chaplain, who busted tail to get it to him as they were about to take off. Irv had no idea how lucky he was, since B-17s routinely carried no extra parachutes.

It took an hour and a half for the bombers on the Augsburg mission to form up. Irv Baum had meticulously checked everything several times. They had been flying about five hours in the number six position, which everybody knew as "coffin corner," when he saw two fighters between six and eight o'clock low, but they disappeared. Several moments later, he looked again and didn't see them. About that time the alarm rang and the plane shuddered slightly. It took a few seconds for the situation to register. They had been hit on the left side and flames were spreading aggressively.

Hooking on his parachute, Baum arrived at the hatch door where Badder stood. Once they released the door, Irv could see the flames beginning to spread. Everything was happening so quickly, even though he felt he was going in slow motion. At that moment, just before he plunged out of the plane, for some reason he thought of the mailman back in his hometown of Monticello, New York.

═══════════

Irv Baum, Bombardier

I counted to ten coming down because it was overcast and undercast, so I wanted to get through the first layer of clouds. As I was coming down, two Fw 190s flew fairly near me but left. Then I heard some shooting but never knew where it was coming from. Once I pulled the rip cord, I continued to fall fast, and as I loped down, I saw an open, plowed field and did my best to maneuver the cords so I could land there.

As soon as I hit down, I looked across the field and recognized Ted Badder about a hundred yards away. We ran toward each other and laid our traces and straps stretched out one way and ran into the woods the other way—it was the only thing we had thought through during the whole thing and we thought it might throw off anyone trying to look for us.

No sooner had we reached the woods than we heard shots and ran into two gendarmes with guns. They pointed them at us and began blowing furiously on their whistles. Within moments, a Volkswagen Kübelwagen, or bucket car, sped up and a captain stepped out. He came up to us and began speaking—in perfect English. I was stunned and could hardly catch my breath.

"Here is how we treat our friends," he said to us and turned and pulled two thousand-franc notes out of his wallet, giving one to each of

the gendarmes. Then he turned and asked us to identify ourselves. When it came my turn, I said my name and then he stared at me for several moments and asked, "Are you Hebrew?" I answered, "No." He said "You're lying," and at the same moment backhanded me across the face with his gloved hand, full force and hard enough to break open the corner of my left eye, a wound which bothers me some even today. It was the day I learned what hatred was.

He must have caught me just right because the blow drove me to the ground and I heard him say "Get into the cart," a small farm wagon which Badder and I decided later was used to haul manure, judging by the smell. I wouldn't have made it in had not Badder dragged me. My face was bleeding pretty badly, and Ted bandaged it as best he could. They drove us into the village of Bronne to a small building that we decided was the mayor's office. We were put into a small room with a table and chairs, and they brought us some bread.

The next day we were put into an old Mercedes with two non-commissioned soldiers. "The war is over for you," one of them said in broken English. They drove us to a fighter base not far away, which they were using as a local brig. One of them came and took off my dirty bandages and cleaned up my face somewhat, applying fresh bandages. After he left my cell, I laid down on the cot, exhausted, and fell asleep almost immediately.

About two o'clock in the morning they jarred me awake and pushed me out of my cell, and I could see they had gotten Badder up as well. It turned out that two very young soldiers were going to Frankfurt on weekend passes and had been given the extra duty of taking two enemy soldiers with them to the central interrogation center there.

When we arrived at the train station, there was a blackout in progress. This part of our situation became almost surreal. These two young soldiers really treated us more like children. They held our hands—there were no handcuffs or anything. I imagined they were probably no more than young teenagers and weren't really sure what to do.

So, I recognized that if I was going to try to get away, this was the time. Once the soldier who was holding my hand let go, I slowly began to back up, edging away from him in the darkness. Suddenly, I backed into something very sharp and thought for sure it was a bayonet. When I turned around it was only a shovel sticking out of somebody's backpack but it caused a commotion. About that time, the soldier who was my guard realized what had happened and had caught up with me. He kept saying over and over, "Nein, nein," but more like he was talking to a child not an enemy combatant. After we boarded the train there were no more opportunities to try to escape.[1]

CHAPTER 7

COGNAC AND EGGS:
DICK MORSE, TAIL GUNNER

December 7, 1941

Dick Morse strolled along the sidewalks of historic St. Augustine, breathing in the salty fresh air on a slow-paced Sunday afternoon, savoring his last few hours of a weekend pass from Camp Blanding, Florida. He had been inducted into the regular army back in February after enlisting in the National Guard in December 1940 at twenty-three years of age in his hometown of Rutland, Vermont. He liked the army well enough but had been thinking recently how he might try to get into flying, which was what he really wanted to do.

Suddenly, several young men came running along the sidewalk and asked if he had heard the news. The Japanese had bombed Pearl Harbor. Morse hurried back to his hotel, and he and the others on weekend passes immediately returned to their base.

The next morning, the entire camp assembled across the company parade ground. Over the loudspeaker came the voice of President Franklin D. Roosevelt, recounting the attack on Pearl Harbor and formally announcing the United States had declared war on Japan. All military personnel would be in the service for the duration of the war plus six months.

Training immediately escalated. Morse went by convoy to Louisiana for the summer, then to North Carolina, and then to Camp Shelby in Hattiesburg, Mississippi, where training became very intense, and he redoubled his efforts to get into flying.

Although two years of college were required for the Army Air Corps, he learned that applicants without this prerequisite could take written and oral tests instead. He didn't pass the first time but waited two months, studied diligently, and passed the second time.

At the classification center for aviation cadets in Nashville, Tennessee, Morse found out he qualified to be a pilot and was sent to pre-flight school at Maxwell Field in Montgomery, Alabama. Here, an extremely regimented training course included eating meals "on the square" in complete silence and running two miles a day in formation. New cadets had to stand at attention, guts sucked in, and if the older cadets didn't like what they saw, they would shorten their belts by cutting off some at the ends.

Finally, the young airman found himself flying a PT-17 Stearman biplane, which had two open cockpits, one for the instructor and one for the student. Communication took place through a Gosport tube. After a few weeks, he was given the thumbs-up to fly solo, which he did several times. Eventually, a major went up with him for a final evaluation. Morse was told more pilots were needed immediately, and there was no time to train any more. So he and more than half the class were washed out.

After taking additional tests, Morse was assigned to be a gunner and sent to armament school at Buckley Field in Denver, Colorado, and at Lowry Field nearby. Then in Salt Lake City, he attended turret school. Finally, in Pyote, Texas, he was assigned the position of tail gunner in a crew with George Wiley Starks as pilot.

On the way to England, flying in daunting weather conditions, Morse thought about how he had never left the United States before. As he headed for a place that was utterly unfamiliar, his new crew suddenly seemed important.

Once in Podington, Morse filled a tail gunner position on two missions with other crews. Then, on March 16, 1944, he was called up for a mission to Augsburg, Germany, this time with his own crew. It was their first mission as a unit since they had been assigned together back in Pyote. The young men felt a certain agitated excitement. At last they were doing what they had been training for months to do — to embark onto the grand stage of World War II in a B-17, their Flying Fortress, their first mission as a *crew together*. None of them had any notion it would be their last.

***

Dick Morse, Tail Gunner

On March 6, 1944, about four a.m., I received a call to report for my first mission to Berlin with a crew that needed a replacement gunner. Our target was the Erkner Ball Bearing Plant. We took off, and as we crossed the English Channel, we fired our guns to test them.

As we approached Berlin, we saw enemy planes in the distance, but they did not attack, and our guns were not fired. We dropped our bombs and encountered a lot of flak, taking a few holes in our plane. Our navigator was hit in the chest, but because he was wearing a flak suit, he wasn't injured. We were gone about eight hours.

On March 8, 1944, I went on my second mission to Berlin with another crew. Although we were not attacked, we saw one of our planes way off in the distance get hit, go into a flat spin, and crash. No one got out.

On March 16, 1944, I was called up for a mission to Augsburg, Germany. This time with my own crew, but with a new co-pilot, because ours had been injured. Our primary target was the Oberpfaffenhofen Dornier Aircraft Plant and an air base was our secondary target. The estimated flight time was ten hours.

After the early morning briefing, we were transported in jeeps to the B-17s, which had been armed and readied during the night. When the departure signal was given, we taxied out single file and took off—one by one—thirty seconds apart. As the lead plane fired a flare, we joined up into a defensive box formation of six planes, lower left corner, called "coffin corner," and then formed the several-hundred-plane bomber stream headed for Germany.

We crossed the English Channel flying over the Strait of Dover, climbed to a twenty-eight-thousand altitude, and received the order, "Test your guns."

When we neared Châlons, France, we saw several fighter planes way off in the distance. As I was scanning the area from my position in the tail of the plane, I glanced to the right, then took a second look. I saw black smoke and flames coming from our wing. Although I didn't hear anything, our number one engine had been hit by a twenty-millimeter shell and exploded. Our gasoline tanks were just behind the engine, and they held thousands of gallons of gas, and we were carrying ten five-hundred-pound HE bombs. I listened for instruction over the intercom and for the warning to exit the plane, but I heard nothing. Our communications was not working. Looking back into the plane, I could see the crew preparing to evacuate.

The flames and black smoke were moving fast and coming towards my window. I could see the framework inside the wing as the aluminum skin melted and pulled away and the fire was coming towards the bomb-bay, which held between two and three tons of bombs.

We were flying at an altitude of approximately twenty-eight thousand feet. In training, we had been told that at this altitude without oxygen a person would lose consciousness in three minutes and in five minutes could be dead. I worked fast—disconnected earphones, throat mike, heated suit cords, and the oxygen supply but left the oxygen mask on my face. It had a corrugated tube about a foot long, and when I grabbed my chest parachute to put it on, it rode up the tube and fell back to the floor. I removed my clumsy gloves—the very same pair our pilot, George Starks, would find twenty-five years later in 1969—and oxygen mask and threw them on the floor, then hooked my parachute on. One last look back through the waist of the plane, I could see the crew putting on their parachutes.

—————

It's not easy to get out of the door on the tail of a B-17 because it is only about two or two and a half feet high, two feet wide, secured with a T-handle between the hinges. I pulled the handle but the door did not budge, so I hit it hard with my fist and it flew off. I was on my knees, put my arms around the chute, and dove out.

When exiting a flying plane, you travel at the same speed the plane is traveling, between two hundred and three hundred miles an hour. I left with a swish and was on my back in a horizontal position. Looking back at the plane, I could see smoke and flames but no one in sight. I had no oxygen with me, so I had to fall rapidly. I was above the clouds and as I floated down through them I tumbled around, but by putting my arms out and spreading my legs, I had some control.

As I came out of the clouds, I was falling fast but felt as if I was not moving at all, though the ground seemed to be coming up. In training, we had received jumping instructions but had never actually jumped from a plane. We had been told not to open our chutes until we could see the windows in houses and there were three reasons for this. At high altitudes (fifty degrees below zero), there would be a lack of oxygen. At our altitude of over five miles, it would be extremely cold and could take twenty minutes to reach the ground, so we would lose consciousness.

Also, *if an enemy pilot saw the parachute, he might strafe it or fly close underneath it, which could suck the air out and collapse it. In addition, waiting to inflate the chute until we were nearer the ground would make it harder for enemies to reach us.*

I couldn't see any buildings but decided it was time to pull the rip cord on my parachute. It was a chest chute, and because they were only twenty-four feet in diameter, they didn't slow you down very quickly. I maneuvered to be on my back so the shroud lines wouldn't cut my face when it opened and then pulled the rip cord. I was falling fast and when the chute opened, it yanked up, bending me backwards, taking my breath away. Though the chute had fully opened, it hadn't slowed me down enough so when I hit the ground I landed very hard, was flipped over, and knocked out for a short time. The last thing I remember before hitting the ground was seeing a very large rabbit running under me. When I came to, I wondered where I was—in France, Alsace Lorraine, or Germany?

It was a beautiful morning—March 16, 1944—about eleven or twelve o'clock. I was on a grassy hill in an open area, and there were a few bushes around. After my hard landing, my back was aching, and looking down the valley, I saw two American planes—a P-47 and a P-51—flying low towards me. Apparently, they had seen my chute and were checking me out. They turned before they got to where I was, however, and flew off in another direction.

I realized I had to do something so I gathered up my chute and crawled into the bushes and lay down. I could hear planes and machine guns, then it was quiet and peaceful, and I could hear church bells in the distance.

My back and legs ached, but I thought I should move on. I covered my chute, a knitted face mask, Mae West vest, and goggles with dirt and dried leaves and started walking. A family in a wagon came down the dirt road, and I hid behind some trees and bushes. They passed about fifty yards from me and were talking, but I couldn't figure out if they were speaking French or German.

In the middle of the afternoon, I was getting really hungry. I hadn't had any food or water since early morning and decided to check my escape kit. It contained a small sewing kit, a compass about the size of a dime, a pint-sized, rubberized bag with a pull string and some halazone tablets to purify water, some new French bills, capsules that could give an evadee energy so he could keep going if he became exhausted while being pursued, a small map of France printed on a folded piece of silk, a few pieces of candy for energy, and a little book with phrases in English with the French version printed across from it.

I stayed hidden until it got dark and using my compass, figured Spain would be to the south and Switzerland to the east. I headed for Switzerland, walking for a while and then lying down to rest. It began to get cold, so I decided it would be better to keep moving. Finally, I came to a large river, maybe the Marne River. I sterilized some water in the rubber bag using the halazone tablets. I walked all night and at about four a.m. came to a field filled with bundles of corn stalks. As I was making a hole in them to crawl into for a little protection, its occupants—dozens of field mice—ran out.

━━━━━━

The next morning, March 17, 1944, I awoke as it began to get light. I was so lame that I could hardly move. I started down a narrow country road and came to an old lumber operation, sat down, lit a cigarette. All I could think about was how much I wished I could let my folks know I was okay. After a few moments, I figured I'd better keep walking.

Before long, an elderly gentleman on a bike came down the road, and I took a chance. I motioned for him to come into the bushes, and he did. I pointed to some of the English sentences in the book from my escape kit, "I am American." "Can you help me?" He became so frightened, he started shaking, didn't say a word to me, and quickly got back on his bike and rode off.

I walked on and soon saw a young man on a bike. I stopped him; he jumped off his bike and shook my hand. He could not speak English, so I pointed to the English words in my book again and he answered "yes" to everything by pointing to the French word. He made a gesture to his chest and said, "Maurice Collette," and motioned to follow him.

He turned his bike around and went ahead. I followed him into a small village where he stopped and motioned me back into some bushes and took off. For a few moments, I felt deep anxiety, not knowing if I could trust this young man or not.

But about twenty minutes later, he was back with some civilian clothes, so I removed my flying clothes and he took them. I also gave him the rip cord that I hadn't dropped when I opened my chute.

After walking a short distance, we came to his house, which was very small, and I surmised the family was quite poor. His mother was in the yard and wore a long, dark dress and wooden shoes. There were some sheep in the yard, and they followed us into the house but were chased out.

Maurice left for work, and his mother prepared toast, eggs, and a beverage for me. I was very thirsty, so I took a big gulp of the beverage, and much to my surprise, it was cognac. Choking, I couldn't catch my breath and ran to the sink, grabbing for the pump. Although I pumped hard and fast, I couldn't get it going, so Collette's mother helped me.

When I had finished eating, she took me to a tiny bedroom where there was a feather bed. I lay down and immediately fell asleep. When I awoke a couple hours later, I was soaking wet with perspiration. For a few seconds I couldn't remember where I was or what had happened exactly.

Then it all rushed back in upon me. I was a long ways from home, in enemy-occupied territory with no idea what would happen next—a very dangerous situation.[1]

CHAPTER 8

MEETING UP WITH BUDDIES: WILLIAM WYATT, BALL TURRET GUNNER, WITH DON EDGERLY, ENGINEER, AND BOB WILLIAMS, RADIO OPERATOR

B ill Wyatt measured only five feet eight inches and weighed 175 pounds, but it was solid muscle. He had been a star athlete at South Hills High School in Pittsburgh on the field and track team, specializing in shotput and javelin, and loved playing baseball.

His upper body strength helped him pull in and out of the ball turret, a thirty-six-inch capsule of plexiglass and thin cast aluminum hanging from the underbelly of the B-17. Two .50 caliber machine guns running completely through the capsule further limited the space. His stocky, muscular form completely filled the interior, and he had to work in a fetal position, with knees pulled up nearly into the chest. A ball turret gunner could be in this position for eight to twelve hours, depending on the length of the mission, and many devised creative ways to relieve themselves using a series of rubber hoses.

Just above the ball turret gunner's shoulders was a small compartment where Bob Williams, the radio operator, sat. Originally from

Manistee, Michigan, he was one of the younger members of the crew, having turned twenty after reaching England. His duties included reporting their position every thirty minutes and assisting the navigator in taking those fixes.

In front of Williams sat the engineer, Don Edgerly, on a sling seat behind the pilot and co-pilot. During a mission, however, the engineer manned the twin guns in the top turret, often first to spot incoming enemy aircraft. Don was five feet six inches tall, weighed 130 pounds, and hailed from Yakima, Washington. When the crew was assembled in Pyote, it became evident that the member with the best sense of humor was Don, who kept the others in stitches with his down-home sayings and quick wit. The day of the Augsburg mission, he was twenty-two years old. The top turret was located ahead of the radio operator, and all three positions—engineer, radio operator, and ball turret gunner— were located approximately mid-ship.

On March 16, 1944, as soon as their B-17 was hit on the left wing, the ball turret began to heat up. Bill Wyatt called to his pilot for permission to leave his position.

"Yes, yes, of course!" George yelled into the intercom. Bill didn't need further urging.

Immediately he began to rotate the turret into a neutral position, the two .50 caliber machine guns pointing downward to allow the hatch to open into the belly of the plane. Bill then began to squeeze his way up and through the small, twenty-four-inch opening. He could feel the plane beginning to pitch, and once inside, he began a frantic search for his chest pack loaded with his parachute. It had slid up against the side of the plane. Grabbing the pack, he quickly clipped it into place on his harness.

Within seconds, Bob Williams, the radio operator, and Don Edgerly, the engineer, were rushing around him, also making sure parachutes were fastened. The three stood for a moment trying to stay balanced as the plane lurched forward. George's voice came over the intercom once more, then went dead in mid-sentence. Immediately the bail out bell rang.

The three crew members hesitated no longer. One of them pulled at the nearest hatch door and a blast of wind tore it from its hinges. Bill braced himself at the opening and then, without another thought, lunged forward into the cold rush of air.

Bill Wyatt, Ball Turret Gunner

The closest large town I landed near was Châlons-sur-Marne, about forty or fifty miles away to the west. I had seen both Don Edgerly and Bob Williams as we were all parachuting down but wind currents took us to different places. I knew, though, they couldn't be too far away.

As soon as I hit, I tried to get out of my chute as fast as possible and hid it in some bushes as best I could. I sat a moment in the trees trying to think and get my bearings. My compass helped me know which direction things were in.

I'd not been down long when I saw a Frenchman dressed in worker's clothes come hurriedly down a path on the other side of a small field. He headed straight for where I was and began whistling softly. I decided to chance it and stood up.

He looked at me a moment, and I indicated I was an American and pointed upward. He nodded his head vigorously. "Oui, oui," he said, then motioned for me to follow him. I really didn't know what else to do—I guess I was still in some kind of shock from the shoot-down and jumping out of the plane, but I followed him.

He took me to a small village nearby. As we walked along, I could see the tiny hamlet was quiet with hardly anyone along the lanes. We arrived at a modest house, and he went straight up to the door and knocked.

A man answered and motioned both of us in. It felt so good to be inside with people I supposed were going to help me. The owner of the house led me to a small parlor kitchen in the back.

"Good grief," I thought, "what on earth is going to happen to me now?" The owner's wife brought me some hot coffee and a roll. It tasted incredible.

That evening, much to my surprise and sheer delight, some other French people brought my radio operator, Bob Williams, to me at this house, and the following evening they brought my engineer, Don Edgerly. We all hugged each other and shook hands like we hadn't seen one another in years.

We talked that night among ourselves as to what to do next. But the owner of the house told us in broken English, "We help, okay?" They gave us a few clothing items to help us look more like the natives and told us we would leave soon. All we could do was trust ourselves to these Frenchmen.[1]

CHAPTER 9

MEETING IN A SHACK: ANDY BRENDEN AND WALLY TRINDER, WAIST GUNNERS

When Arden Brenden, one of ten children born to John and Anne Brenden, left Starbuck, Minnesota, he was barely twenty years old and had never been out of his county. Called Andy by family and friends, he joined the Army Air Corps and was assigned as a waist gunner on B-17s.

After training, Andy arrived at Pyote Army Air Field for combat training. Once he was assigned to the crew of George Starks, he met the other waist gunner, Wallace "Wally" Trinder, a Massachusetts native who quickly became known as "Pops," since at twenty-seven he was the old man of the group.

Andy and Wally got along well and kept up friendly bantering while practicing their firing techniques. Their positions as left and right waist gunners in the B-17 kept them standing back-to-back at slightly off-set mountings of their .50 caliber machine guns.

Both had flown as fill-ins for other missions, but on March 16, 1944, they were excited about their first mission with the crew they had trained to fly with. When the plane was hit and the left wing burst into flames, both hurried toward the rear door on the right side. Wally tried to pry the hatch door off but the slipstream pushed against it with such force he couldn't budge it. So Andy began kicking it violently with his foot.

Andy Brenden, Waist Gunner

I don't suppose I've been as afraid in all my life as when the door of our B-17 flew off and I looked downward into wide open spaces. The fear of jumping into uncertainty was horrible.

During one of our instruction classes in parachuting, one of the students asked the instructor, "Well, now what if I pull the string and this thing doesn't open?" Our instructor replied, "That is what you call jumping to a conclusion."

When I started tumbling down I blacked out a little, but once I hit the clouds the moisture actually felt good. Looking down swinging in the chute, everything below seemed so peaceful and quiet—it was hard to imagine people below were fighting and dying.

As I neared the ground, I looked over and saw a little church. They were having a wedding and everybody stopped and looked up at me. The wind blew me into a field next to a wooded area. I hit hard in a dirt rut with too much pressure on my left foot and damaged the bones and arch but hobbled to hide my parachute.

Then I quickly entered a little ways into the wooded area and covered myself up with branches and debris and lay that way for several hours. I could hear motorcycles going up and down the roadway—Germans looking for all of us who had parachuted into the area.

Later in the afternoon, I noticed an older lady walking through the fields with a small sack, but I was too afraid to make any noise or indicate I was there. She made her way over to a small wooden shack not far away and set down the sack.

When she left, I went over to it and found a couple pieces of hard bread and a little meat. I didn't know whether she had gone to tell the Germans or not. I feel certain she knew I was there.

That night after dark, she came back with a bottle of wine, cigarettes, and a little more food. She had two girls with her I assumed were her daughters, and they saw me at the shack in my flight uniform—so the woman knew I was an American. Not saying a word she just left the provisions and went away again with the girls. As she left, I could sense that she was possibly as afraid as I was because she had much at stake if she should happen to get caught doing the things she did for me. I slept out in the woods that night, because I didn't want to be surprised inside the shack and waited.[1]

Wally Trinder, Waist Gunner

I followed Andy out of the plane and delayed opening my chute and calculated I had come down probably about three hundred yards away from him. When I landed, I really hurt my back but managed to get to the woods and hid until dark.

Then I crossed a small field and a narrow stream and into a swampy area, then soon came across a man cutting wood. He recognized me as an American flyer at once, and motioned for me to hide in the brush. Shortly he returned with food and clothing. He made me understand that I should remain where I was because there were Germans everywhere.

I spent the night in the swamp and in the morning took off southwards by compass across another field. About noon I approached another solitary worker, who gave me a piece of bread he had in his sack and warned me to avoid the roads. That night I slept in a patch of woods and early the next morning I took up my hike again.

That morning I found someone else working in a field and asked him whether the region was safe. He gave me directions, and I walked off but hadn't gone very far when he called me back. He told me he knew where one of my friends was located.

I was a little apprehensive, but I had no other choice that I could see. So I walked a little ways behind him across the field.[2]

As Wally followed the Frenchman, he realized they were re-entering the woods. When they neared a small hut, the Frenchman waved the American forward.

Wally carefully cracked open the door and there, to his relief and surprise, stood Andy Brenden.

"Hey, Wally, great to see you," said Andy and the two men shook hands vigorously. "I thought I saw you coming down, but you were too far away for me to get to you. Besides, I busted my foot when I landed."

Wally looked down at Andy's badly swollen foot. "It looks pretty bad. Do you think it's broken?"

"Feels like something cracked maybe," said Andy. "It's great to have you here. Let's just make a pact to stick together no matter what. Okay?"

Wally agreed. They both settled down and slept fitfully through the night.

The next morning the Frenchman returned to the hut with work clothes for each of them. He knew a little English, and Wally remembered some French from a college course. Between the two, Wally determined he was a plasterer.

The Frenchman made them understand there were Germans all around in the woods. They needed to leave and follow a small river into the next village. He pulled a crudely drawn map from his pocket and pointed to a small bridge where they would meet someone who would hide them and get help for Andy's foot.

The two airmen quickly changed into their French workmen's clothing and handed over their flight suits and .45 revolvers. Thanking the plasterer for all his help and reminding him to thank the woman and her daughters for the food and cigarettes, they began their journey deeper into the woods.

CHAPTER 10

A CASKET AND A BICYCLE: GEORGE STARKS

I continued walking south, avoiding the main roads when possible, sticking to smaller country lanes that mostly paralleled the highways. When food, rest, or sleep was needed, I tried farmhouses that stood alone or with woods nearby, in case I needed to escape quickly.

Most of the people would help; they were real heroes. They gave me a share of whatever meager food they had. Usually it was a piece of black bread or a bit of cheese, and of course, wine—cut half-and-half with water.

One woman boiled some eggs for me—a sacrifice. Another gave me some sugar cubes for energy—an even greater sacrifice. And no one in France would take any of the francs from my escape kit for payment—no one.

Any who helped me did so at terrible risk to themselves. Any French civilian caught helping a downed Allied airman was summarily taken out of his house by the Germans and shot—man, woman, child, it made *no difference. If there had been a recent reprisal in the area, of course, the farmhouse would turn me away. I understood.*

Anyway…I rested where I could, ate where I could, slept where I could. I had shortened my day's walking now to only twelve or fifteen kilometers. If there was no willing farmhouse once night arrived—and it was still bitter cold—I would burrow down into a haystack. I'll tell you right now, though, you do not sleep in a haystack—you simply pass the night away.

It was during this time, before I reached Chaumont even, that depression began to creep in. I was constantly cold and tired and without adequate food or rest to replenish me against the stress and exertion.

And too, I was picking up enough French to understand full well the opinions of people I spoke to: "Switzerland? Impossible! Too far…too much snow…too many Germans…the mountains. What? You don't ski! How do you expect to reach Switzerland?"

I was alone, scared, not knowing who would help, not knowing who might turn me over to the Germans. Glimmers of hope would come and then quickly fade. My one, constant hope was that I'd run into the French Underground, but there was no way to contact them. You just had to bump into them, and this didn't seem to be happening.

My mental resilience was sinking with my physical condition. I gave thoughts to turning myself in, becoming a POW. But I was out of uniform and in civilian clothes and wasn't sure what they would do to me.

Those thoughts made me push on, again and again. And at that time, I had no idea of the terrible and telling despondency that I would later face in the mountains.

Anyway, I kept walking south toward Chaumont….[1]

When George reached the outskirts of Chaumont, he was tired, hungry, and discouraged. It seemed like months since his B-17 had been shot down, and the foot and thigh wounds he had suffered continued to hinder him.

Under the circumstances, it was not surprising that at the town's edge he made his first serious mental mistake. The thought of having to detour through thick woods to bypass the village was overwhelming. So on a split-second's decision, he decided to walk straight through.

As George began making his way along the narrow sidewalks, he realized he had made a catastrophic error. Almost immediately he saw several soldiers on foot and sentries standing outside buildings displaying Nazi flags. He was considering turning around and hastily retreating when two trucks filled with soldiers rumbled past. He had no choice now but to continue walking into the heart of the downtown area.

Leafless trees lined the cobblestone street, and a chilly wind blew through the tunnel formed by two-story buildings on both sides. Pulling his jacket collar around his face, he dug his hands into his jacket and tried to walk with a sense of purpose.

When he reached an opening that allowed him to peer between the buildings, he saw what appeared to be a German fighter base across the road in the field beyond. George spotted several Me 190s parked in revetments under camouflage netting. "No wonder this place is crawling with Germans," thought George. "Of all the towns for me to go through. What was I thinking?"

Adrenaline kept his mind focused as he continued along the side-walk. Since it was mid-morning, most shops were already open. Suddenly the door to a small café swung open, and the aroma of coffee and fresh bakery items reminded him how empty his stomach was. Even though he was starving, he dared not stop.

A bit farther along, he came to a small square opposite a row of townhouses. The long red flags hanging on its façade indicated that it was occupied by German officers. A horse-drawn wagon waited in front of one of the doors, and a field grade officer stood on the front steps. When he spotted George across the street, the officer immediately made a stern motion with his arms for him to come over.

George's heart jumped to his throat; he stood frozen. The officer yelled something out in German that George didn't understand and signaled with his hand again, his face now scowling with impatience. There was nothing to do but walk over and see how it played out.

As George crossed the road, several soldiers in Luftwaffe uniforms spilled out the front door, struggling to maneuver a large wooden box through the narrow townhouse opening and down the steps. When he reached the group, he realized the box they were carrying was a coffin. At that moment, the officer barked something else to him and began motioning for George to help load the coffin up onto the wagon. Having no choice, he squeezed in between two of the soldiers and with trembling hands helped to hoist the coffin.

The officer extended no "thank you" for his help, and George didn't stick around to receive any. Once the task was completed, he stepped back and turned to walk away. He shoved his hands into his pockets, hoping the others didn't notice how badly they were shaking. As he walked off, he was certain he could sense the officer staring at his back. About that moment, he heard one of the soldiers yell something and whistle. George kept walking. Then he heard the squeak of wagon wheels as the horse pulled away from the sidewalk. The Germans must have been focused on the task at hand, because no one called out to the young evadee.

George quickened his steps to put as much distance as he could between himself and those Luftwaffe airmen with their casket. "I'll bet that German officer didn't speak any French," he thought to himself. "Good thing for me because all the French I know is 'Je suis pilote américain—partais à Suisse.' Doubt he would have been amused at that!" For the first time since he had been shot down, George chuckled to himself.

As he walked along, he continued to think about the incident. "That may have been a casualty from the fighter base in the coffin," he thought. "Man, what a close call! Too close." He wished more than ever that he could make contact with someone who could really help him, maybe the French Underground or the Resistance.

When he came to the other side of Chaumont, he noticed an unattended bicycle leaning against one of the last buildings. He hated to steal it, but suddenly his legs felt like logs. He knew he couldn't walk much further. Glancing around to see if anyone was watching, he hopped on, pumping rapidly to get out of town.

Very quickly he was cycling through rolling countryside. He wondered what had happened to the others in his crew. Were they trying to get to Switzerland, had they found people to help them, or had they been captured? A darker thought entered his mind: had any of them been killed? So many unknowns....

Worn out, the young pilot looked at the deceptively peaceful landscape of cultivated fields on both sides of the road and mountains far in the distance—beautiful to look at, he thought, but how in the world would he get across them? No choice now but to continue pedaling in a southward direction.

PART III

THE HELPERS
AND THE ENEMY

CHAPTER 11

PROCESSING IN FRANKFURT AM MAIN: IRV BAUM AND TED BADDER

I rv and Ted, still under escort by the two very young German soldiers, finally arrived by train at Frankfurt am Main and were taken to the *Dulag Luft* approximately eight miles northwest of the city for interrogation and processing.[1] By late 1943, more than a thousand prisoners of war were passing through there a month. In 1944, that number rose to an average of two thousand per month and reached a peak in July 1944 of more than three thousand.

A large stone building that looked more like a municipal office was originally used for interrogating and holding POWs, and there were solitary confinement cells for all incoming prisoners. The entire compound was surrounded by heavy wire fencing, with guards patrolling round the clock.

After the crewmates arrived, they were separated and placed in single cells. The young servicemen stayed together and placed their cardboard suitcases on two side-by-side bunks. "Take care," said Ted to Irv as they were led off in different directions.

But about ten o'clock, sirens began to blare as the RAF began bombing runs over the compound. Since the barracks were not marked as housing for POWs, they became targets.

Immediately the guards rushed all prisoners into two rather small underground bunkers, one for officers and one for enlisted men. As the men in Irv's and Ted's bunker listened to the explosions above ground, one hit fairly close to the opening, and a beam holding up part of the bunker came crashing down, crushing the skull of a young American officer who had been leaning against it. The guards then hustled everyone into the bunker holding enlisted men. Now there were so many POWs in one bunker, there was no room to sit down. Men were locked in here the rest of the day and all night without food or toilets.

When they were finally released from the bunker, dozens of townspeople stood against the wire fences shaking their fists and screaming at the POWs. Ted and Irv both agreed that if the populace could get their hands on them, they would be killed.

Irv Baum

At the interrogation center near Frankfurt, they took away every-thing, our belts, trousers, shoes, socks—even my class ring, but I did get that back. After about three days, they gave me my trousers back. All of us were in separate cells, so no one really knew what was happening to anybody else.

My cell was long and narrow with only a cot. We were fed chicory coffee and toast but that's about it. After I had been there about two days, I was taken to another building to meet for the first time an inter-rogator. I was apprehensive, not really knowing what to expect.

The room they led me into had a big desk, and this really fine look-ing officer sat there scanning papers. Once I had been seated in front of him, he said, "Good morning, Mr. Baum," again in the most perfect

English I've ever heard, with the exception of the officer who had broken open my eye.

He continued, "I see you are from Monticello. I used to live in Middleton." That was a town not more than twenty-five miles from my hometown. I couldn't believe it. Then came the question that shocked me almost out of my mind. This German officer asked, "Is Mr. Rutherford still the principal there?"

We had always heard that the German interrogators were smart and would try to use different techniques to soften you or make you feel comfortable. But this had just the opposite effect—I couldn't believe it. We also learned that they had lots of interrogators who knew about different places in the states, and once they knew where you were from, they would tap an officer who was familiar with your area to interrogate you.

He went on to say he actually lived in the United States and had come back to Germany to visit an aunt when the war broke out and he couldn't get back to the states. Then he said something that gave me a complete chill. He said, "We are going to get you Americans to do something you don't do—and that is to tell the truth." With that, he waved a guard to take me back to my cell. I just collapsed on my cot trying to make sense of it all.

The next morning they took me back to him. "We have ways to make you tell the truth. Remember, Mr. Baum, we have guards who don't like Jews." His line of questioning had been about who had been with me in the plane that had been shot down and I kept saying it was a crew I didn't usually fly with, so I didn't know any of them. Then it was back to my cell.

About midnight, a guard shook me awake and pushed me out the cell door into the passageway. I saw Badder down the hall—the first time I had seen him since we had been there. There were about five of us they were taking outside, including a guy from Oklahoma named Walter Beckham, who was one of our leading P-47 aces.

They marched us out into the courtyard—it was a black night, cold, windy, and they told us to line up across one end of the yard. Then six or seven guards came out with rifles and an officer with a sword. Somebody said, "Holy Christ, this is a firing squad." And as they lined up in front of us, the officer yelled "Ready…Aim…Fire!" But nothing happened. They put us back into our cells and I spent a sleepless night, trying to control wave after wave of nausea.

Later that same morning they came and got us and we headed for the train on foot. It's hard to describe what it's like being under complete control of the enemy. I had no idea where we were going. None of us did.[2]

Ted Badder

When it came time to leave the processing camp, we had to march to the train station. Several guys were really hurt, so they loaded them in a bus, but the rest of us had to hoof it.

We walked about six abreast, and all along the roads women came up on bicycles and threw garbage on us, screaming and yelling—one farmer ran at us with his pitchfork. There were about two hundred of us, and we walked so long my feet were burning like fire. When we finally arrived at the train station, it felt good just to sit down. Irv and I tried to stay together—it was comforting to know you had a buddy alongside you.

Before we left, however, we had each been given a cardboard suitcase—I guess the Red Cross provided them. At any rate, they contained pajamas, a toothbrush with small tubes of toothpaste, and small shaving kits. Somehow I was proud of my suitcase—it seemed extravagant after realizing I didn't have anything else. It was funny how guys protected them.

The ride deeper into Germany was okay, but we worried about our fighters shooting at us. We were pretty sure the train was not marked. We rode into Berlin and then kept going.

After riding for several hours, we pulled right up to a large compound. As we got off the train, we were greeted by a German officer who said in perfect English, "Gentlemen, this is your new home—Stalag Luft III—owned and operated by the Luftwaffe."[3]

CHAPTER 12

LIVING WITH THE VIDELS: DICK MORSE

Dick Morse rested for most of the day at the small farm belonging to the mother of the young man who had spotted him in the woods—the woman who had introduced him to cognac and eggs. She worked around their cottage sweeping and cleaning, feeding their cow, and tending their few sheep. He gathered they were struggling to live on very meager means.

The young pilot found that as long as he was up and moving around, he was all right, but as soon as he sat down, he would doze off. He realized the crash and events of the past couple of days had been more traumatic than he had thought.

When Maurice Collette returned home from work, they had rabbit for dinner, which was considered a delicacy. Dick wondered if someone else had given the meat to them. Through sign language and by using Dick's small French dictionary, Maurice managed to tell him that in two days a man by the name of Dr. Fritch would come to the farm. He was a member of the French Underground and would help Dick on his way. Though Dick felt nervous about the situation, he had no reason to doubt the young man so far.

In a couple of days, the doctor arrived on a motorcycle. Middle-aged and well dressed in leather puttees and jacket, he spoke good English. Dick showed him his French money, brand new bills that had been part of his survival kit. Cautioning Dick that such crisp bills might arouse suspicion, Dr. Fritch took all the money and left. The next day he returned with worn bills of equivalent value. The doctor explained that early the next day, while it was still dark, Dick would leave the farm with Maurice Collette. Dick's sleep that night was fitful: he kept thinking about tomorrow and what might happen.

Dick Morse

At about four a.m., Maurice came in to wake me up, but I wasn't asleep. We left the cottage, and Maurice walked ahead of me. He said if he whistled, it would be a warning and I should duck into the bushes. We walked for about two hours on roads and across fields and finally saw a truck. Maurice whistled and I hurried into the bushes.

He spoke to the man in the truck and then brought me to him. Maurice and I said our good-byes. I thanked him, we shook hands, and I never saw him again.

The man in the truck turned out to be the village butcher in the town of Orconte, some distance away. He took me to his home, where his wife gave me something to eat and then took me to a nice bedroom where I lay down. Every now and then the door would open quietly and someone would peek in. I believe they were friendly neighbors who had just stopped by and wanted to see the American airman.

I stayed at this house for two days; then the butcher brought a woman to meet me. Her name was Margo Videl. She spoke a little English and told me she was going to take me to her house where I could stay. I followed her outside to her car, where her driver waited. We got inside and drove to her home, which was about twenty miles away in the town of Saint-Vrain.

When I arrived there, Margo introduced me to two other guys, who she said were staying there also. They said their names were Dick Krecher and Ken Downey, and they had been shot down the same day that I was, March 16, in the same area but with a different group.

They both looked like Germans to me, and although they asked me many questions for about a week, I was very careful not to give them any information.[1]

———

Jean and Margo Videl, a couple in their early thirties, lived with their three young daughters, Jacelyn, ten, Denise, six, and Michelle, four, in a large two-story building at the edge of town. Their sprawling house with its oversized rooms was well-known in the area since Jean, a teacher, used one of the first-floor rooms as a schoolroom for Saint-Vrain. He was also well connected with the mayor and other town leaders, who often met with German officers in an upstairs drawing room. As a result, people were constantly flowing in and out of the house. This activity actually served as a convenient cover for hiding American soldiers. The Germans would hardly suspect someone who openly allowed the enemy to conduct business in his home.

Yet the Videls knew full well the great risk they were taking. They asked the American soldiers to stay in their own small room and use the kitchen exclusively for washing and shaving. This they were to do only when their children were gone or occupied in another area of the large house. Since no one was supposed to be living in that part of the house, they didn't build a fire in their room because the smoke might be spotted and arouse suspicions. At night, the shutters all over the house were kept shut tight.

The Americans were not allowed outside except late at night, again a precaution for all concerned. Two or three armed Frenchmen would accompany the three young men so they could get exercise and walk around. Jean had a shack hidden deep in the woods, and the armed Frenchmen told them if they ever needed to hide, that was where they should go.

As far as Dick was aware, the Videl children never knew soldiers were being sequestered in a remote part of their house. Even the mayor himself did not know their secret. The mayor's son did, however, and brought extra bags of flour to Margo to help with baking for the additional mouths she was feeding.

A neighbor girl named Monique Ruppeno would often come over to help sift the flour in the Videls' storage room. Dick enjoyed her company and helped her with the sifting. Sometimes Jean would peek into the small room to check on their progress. Dick got the idea he was really just making sure the two of them were keeping their minds on bread making.

Occasionally in the evenings, after the children were in bed, the Videls would ask two or three trusted friends over to visit. Dick and the other Americans loved talking with these townspeople. One of them thought Dick looked like Charles Lindbergh, which pleased him immensely since he was a great admirer of the famous aviator.

For safety, the young airmen were instructed not to open the door when the Videls were away unless they heard a certain knock: dot-dot-dot, pause, dot. One day when Dick was shaving in the kitchen, he thought he had heard the signal. He stopped pulling the razor across his face, motionless for a moment. Then the knock came again. He listened carefully; it was their code, so he opened the door. There stood a strange man Dick had never seen before. Shocked and horrified, he quickly slammed the door shut. He decided not to tell the Videls—nothing could be done about it anyway—but he worried himself nearly sick for several days and prayed it wouldn't result in something devastating. To his relief, nothing ever came of it.

After several weeks, three more airmen arrived, one named Joe Wagner. Dick and Joe quickly became close friends. But now there were six grown men being hidden in the house—everyone knew it was time to move on.

For such a journey, many preparations had to be made by the French Underground. Photos were taken of the young Americans for fake passports, and each needed authentic civilian clothing. Dick's passport described him as a Polish deaf mute cabinetmaker.

Since extracting all six simultaneously would attract too much attention, the Underground said they needed to draw straws to see which three would go first. The men drawing the longest straws would leave, then the other three would follow one week later.

Dick, Joe, and Ken, one of the men Dick previously thought was a German, drew the longest straws. They were told they would be taken to a train station the following morning by a guide, then another contact would travel with them to another destination, from which they would walk over the Pyrenees Mountains into Spain. They were given a secret code that could be broadcast by radio to notify the Underground once they were successful.

Dick and Joe whispered to each other that evening. "This looks like it's the real deal," said Dick. "I guess I'm glad, but I also hate to leave here."

"Yeah—I know what you mean," said Joe. "It's been good to have a place to sleep and meals too. Wish we knew what was going to happen in the next few days. But we're with the Underground, and they sure seem to know what they're doing."

Both men tried to remain optimistic about leaving the Videls. Their gratitude for what had been done for them was deep and heartfelt. But they knew it was impossible for all six of them to continue to stay there. What lay ahead was anybody's guess.[2]

CHAPTER 13

"GET THE HELL OUT OF HERE": DICK MORSE CONT'D

Dick Morse, along with his new buddy Joe Wagner and Ken, the other airman, had been instructed to follow their guide at a distance. When he stopped to speak to a certain person, they were to follow the next helper to the train station. The person they were following bought tickets and discreetly gave one to each American. They boarded the train separately but kept one another in sight. When the train reached Vitry-le-François, they followed their guide down a narrow street to a small house and gave the door three quick raps followed by a pause and one more knock. The door opened slightly, and the three men slipped inside.

It was the home of a French soldier who had been captured at the battle of Dunkirk in May 1940, escaped, and returned to Vitry to help Allies escape. He shook hands enthusiastically with the three American evadees, then he handed Dick a ledger to sign, a record of who had come through the Underground network. Dick looked down at the list and couldn't believe what he saw. "Hey, guys, will you look at this?" he exclaimed. "Here's the names of two of my crewmen, Andy Brenden and Wally Trinder." Dick was thrilled to see they had survived the crash and not been captured, but he couldn't believe the coincidence.

"When were they here?" Dick asked the French soldier.

"About two months ago. I saw your plane go down in a ball of fire. It was several kilometers away, but we were able to make contact with them fairly quickly," he explained. He spoke with a heavy French accent but could be understood.

The news raised Dick's spirits as nothing else had done since their B-17 had been shot down.

The Frenchman continued, "One of your crew, the one called Andy, had hurt his ankle badly when he landed. We were able to get him some aid before the Underground took them both to Paris. From there, we hoped to get them to Spain by walking through the Pyrenees. We will try to do the same for all of you." Dick was elated. It gave him and his companions confidence to know that the network had been able to help Andy and Wally. Things seemed more solid now.

They spent one day and a night in that house, then followed their guide to the train station. It was time to leave for Paris. The train arrived after an uneventful trip at a crowded station. It was an afternoon in the middle of May, and people were evacuating Paris hastily because an Allied invasion was expected.

In the crush of people, the young Americans lost their guide. They didn't know what to do, so they just started walking along the edge of the trains. Suddenly a man came up behind them and said quietly, "Follow me." Dick and the other two men spread out and tried to keep the Frenchman in sight. Soon he went up to another person, shook hands with him, and Dick figured this was a signal now to tag behind the new guide.

In the noisy crowd Joe and Ken became separated from Dick, so he followed several people and eventually tagged behind a young girl to the top floor of a building not far from the train station. When Dick followed her into the upstairs room, there were Joe and Ken sitting with an older lady.

"Gees, am I glad to see you guys," said Dick. They were all nervous after this experience and sat down on the floor away from the windows. The girl left, returning a while later with a small satchel. She had brought them each a change of clothing and signaled for them to stay there overnight.

At about five a.m., the older woman awakened the three airmen, instructing them to walk back to the train station and look for a young girl wearing an unusual hat. "Plans have changed. You will not be traveling to Bordeaux. In the night, a trestle was blown up and the train must detour. Watch the girl, and she will direct you to a man in a car. Be very careful. Germans are watching everyone."

Even at that early hour, the young men found the train station packed. They separated slightly and looked around for a girl wearing an unusual hat. Dick spotted a small, pretty girl—she looked more like a teen than a woman—wearing a hat with feathers that flowed down one side nearly touching her shoulders. He presumed she was their guide.

When he got on the train, he had to sit on the floor in the aisle because it was so crowded. As they rode along, several men—Dick couldn't tell if they were French—tried to talk to him, but he pretended he was a deaf-mute. At about one o'clock, he saw Joe get up and head for the door, and he saw Ken getting off at the other end of the car. Dick quickly stood up and stepped over people to get off. But there were so many people on the platform, he couldn't find the girl or Joe or Ken.

Looking around, he nervously pondered the prospect of being alone in the town of Niort—he had seen the train station sign. All he knew was that it was four hours or so south of Paris. Now, after the long train ride, Dick needed a restroom. He found one, where he was immediately joined by a German soldier. He got out as quickly as possible and to his relief, found Joe and Ken together on a bench. They whispered to him that they had seen the girl get off the train, buy some bread, and re-board, headed back to Paris. The three young men looked at each other, not sure what to do. They realized something must have gone wrong.

Leaving the train station, they found another bench, where they quietly talked over their situation and wondered what in the world they were going to do. Suddenly, a man came up behind them, leaned over Dick's shoulder, and in perfect English said, "If I was you guys, I'd get the hell out of here." He turned and walked off quickly, disappearing around the corner of a building.

The three young men needed no further prompting. Though they had no idea who the man was or where he had come from, they knew he was American, or perhaps English, and they quickly began walking rapidly along the first road they could find, heading south until they reached the outskirts of Niort. They kept on walking until late in the evening, when they came to a small abandoned house a little ways off the road. They collapsed inside for the night, tired and hungry.

The next morning we got up and studied the silk map we had, trying to figure out how to get to Spain. In training we had been told if we needed direction or help our best bet would be to ask railroad men, but there were no railroads around.

We traveled back roads and across fields and slept in barns and abandoned buildings. Occasionally we stopped at a farmhouse and asked for food. Sometimes we were given a couple of slices of bread, perhaps some coffee, but many times the door was not opened, or if it was, it closed very quickly. Either they had no food or they were afraid to help us.

After the three of us had traveled together for several days, Ken, who was older than Joe and me, said he didn't like the idea of all of us traveling together. He felt we would do better if we split up.

We asked him what he was going to do, and he said he was going to try to find an axe and look like a woodsman. I never saw him again but later heard he was captured in southern France, then escaped.

After he left us, Joe and I talked about it and decided we definitely wanted to stay together.

As we walked along the next day, we saw a group of Germans at a distance and they spotted us. They began firing their guns at us, so we ran into the woods and hid. After several hours, they evidently gave up trying to find us, and we moved on.

By this time we were really hungry, but we knew we had to keep pushing southward. We crossed a large river, and when we reached the other side two large dogs chased us up a thorny tree, where we stayed about an hour until we were sure they had gone.

Later that afternoon, we came to a village where there was a man near a barn. We were starving and decided to chance going up to him and asking for food. When we did, he seemed friendly and invited us into the barn where several huge casks of wine were lined up in a row.

He offered some to us and then filled the little bag from my escape kit. While we were standing in front of the barn talking, a woman ran down the path to us screaming, "Partez, messieurs, partez!" She was followed by a young woman with a dark green scarf tied around her head.

The man looked stricken and said we should leave immediately. He told us to take the path into the woods until we came to a dirt road. We should travel along the dirt road about a half-mile, then we would see an abandoned mill where we could stay for the night.

We did what he told us, running down into the forest. We found the old mill, overgrown with bushes. By this time it was about five o'clock in the afternoon but a beautiful day.

Joe told me he was so tired and hungry that he felt weak. We both were and had had a rough couple of days. We checked around to make sure everything seemed all right, and I hung my little bag of wine on a stake near the doorway. Then we both lay down on the grass and went right to sleep.

I hadn't been asleep very long when I heard voices talking. I jerked awake, and four German soldiers had their rifles pointed down at us. I stood up quickly with my hands raised. My heart was pounding so fast I could hardly breathe.

Joe was still asleep. One of the Germans kicked his foot and he started to move.

"Get up, Joe," I said to him. "We've been captured."[1]

CHAPTER 14

SITTING AROUND A FRENCH FIREPLACE: BILL WYATT, DON EDGERLY, AND BOB WILLIAMS

The day after their reunion, Wyatt, Edgerly, and Williams were led by one of the Frenchmen to the next small town, Vavray-le-Grand, where he told them that another person would meet them along the street and take them to a nearby house. Then he turned and walked off hastily.

Now they were not certain how to proceed. "I guess we just keep walking along," said Don. As they entered the outskirts of the town, they took a chance and spoke to a man they passed along a deserted side street.

Shaking his head, he kept walking past them. But in a few minutes, they noticed he had turned around and was looking at them. Don Edgerly nudged Bob.

"I'll bet you a horse turd to a dollar he is the one who is going to help us. And I'll hold the stakes in my teeth." It was one of Don Edgerly's favorite sayings. The other two had heard their crewmate say it many times since they first met him in Pyote. Don had always been the one with a great sense of humor and hilarious sayings, keeping the other crewmen in stitches most of the time.

The man did indeed come toward them, saying nothing, and gestured for them to follow him. They decided to take a chance and fell in behind him, but at a distance. The Frenchman picked up his pace and headed down a small lane lined with two-story residential buildings, ending in a cul-de-sac of three or four small houses. He walked around to the rear of one, the young Americans tagging along, opened the back door, looked back, and motioned for them to come in quickly.

They found themselves in a small parlor with a whitewashed brick fireplace. A fire was already burning, and its warmth felt good in the chilly air. The gentleman pulled several ladderback chairs from a small kitchen table and pushed them toward the hearth. "Asseyez-vous," he said and pointed to the chairs. Bill and Bob both wasted no time stretching their hands toward the fire.

At that moment, a woman they supposed was his wife appeared from one of the front rooms. She greeted them, speaking in French interspersed with a little English. Don began to explain who they were. "Je suis américain."

"Oui, oui," the man said. "You fly and crash," he said, motioning with his hands. "We know."

With the little French the young men had picked up and the little English the couple knew, they were able to make introductions. The Americans' next helpers were Gérard Lambert and his wife, Simone. They lived in this house with their young son, Pierre. The couple told the men they could stay in a small room upstairs for a couple of days, but they had to be careful to keep away from the windows.

The Lamberts asked the Americans if they had photos of themselves. Each man had a picture of himself in civilian clothes tucked inside his survival kit. Gérard told them he might be able to get papers that resembled work permits, which would help them should they be stopped and questioned. The crewmen handed their photos to Gérard, who carefully put them inside his shirt and left to work on the documents.

That evening when all of them gathered around the fire, Gérard told the Americans he might have some false identification papers for them in a couple of days. They could stay in his house until then. The airmen, who desperately needed rest before pushing forward, were overjoyed.

While they were there, young Pierre was intent on learning a little English. The three Americans took turns teaching him a few words, but it was Don who seemed especially eager to tutor his young protégé. He began with some basic words of greeting, but before long he was teaching the boy baseball terms. Pierre seemed to like that part of his English lessons the best.

In two days, Gérard returned with forged papers and the original photos. Having duplicated their pictures, he told the airmen that he and Simone would keep them with their family photos so they could remember them always.

On the third morning, the three men knew it was time to depart. Shaking hands with the couple, Bill said, "We really thank you for this."

"Stay away from big towns," Simone said. "And keep heading south. Maybe you will be able to contact the Underground."

Agreeing that they would sorely miss the Lamberts with their warm fireplace and curious little Pierre eager to learn a few English words, the three Americans said their good-byes and headed south.

"Hey," said Bob to the other two, "what do you think happened to Starks and the other guys?"

"Don't know. Hope they made it. But I'm sure glad we have each other right now," said Bill.

CHAPTER 15

AN ENGINEER'S HOME, A DRESS SHOP, AND A ROOT CELLAR: ANDY BRENDEN AND WALLY TRINDER

Andy Brenden

Wally and I started out the morning of the fourth day we were down, hobbling along the river. It was extremely foggy, which was to our advantage, and we came to the small village of Vitrele François.

There we spotted the bridge through the trees where we were supposed to meet our contact, but no one showed up. We decided to continue on and hid nearby in the brush just waiting to see what would develop.

Later in the afternoon, we lay down and fell asleep. It was dark when I woke up, and the moon was shining down through the wooded area. I thought for sure it was a German spotlight. I jumped up screaming but quickly realized what I had done. So Wally and I hid further back into the brush.

*But my screams drew some attention in the village, and a lady came
down to the river with a bucket pretending to get water. We decided to
take a chance and called over to her saying quietly, "Americans. Americans." She got on her bicycle and rode over the bridge to us, then motioned
for us to follow her at a distance.*[1]

Mme. Lisette Meyers was a pleasant, slightly-built woman in her late
thirties. She lived in a farmhouse with an attached barn on the outskirts of
the village of Ponthion with her twelve-year-old daughter, Jacqueline. Her
husband had been placed in a German work camp as a prisoner of war.

When Mme. Meyers realized how badly injured Andy's foot was,
she sought help—in the form of an elderly veterinarian. The Americans
looked at each other with a shrug of the shoulder, and Andy sat down
on the floor. The vet pulled a jar of liniment from his satchel and rubbed
it all over the swollen foot. Within a few seconds the throbbing began to
ease. "I guess it's working," said Andy, looking up and smiling. "Thanks."

The vet seemed pleased to help. He nodded and left the hut.

Andy Brenden

*We stayed in Mme. Meyers's barn for nearly three weeks. She was
a wonderful, wonderful woman. But our being there was a tremendous
hardship on her. She was very much afraid all the time, and with the lack
of food due to rationing in France she was much inconvenienced. Other
people in the village helped out with food, including a young man named
Gaston and a woman who worked for the French Red Cross.*

*One evening when Germans were patrolling the street, she got wor-
ried and put us in the cellar where she stored wine and other strong
spirits. With nothing else to do, Wally and I tapped into them.*

*Needless to say we became quite vocal and loud. We tried to open
the trap door, but she had locked us in for good reason. She didn't need
loud Americans in her living room with Germans outside.*

After this she became very frightened and thought we should leave. But we had no idea where to go. We both felt if we just walked out on the highway it would only be a matter of time before we would end up in a concentration camp.

We begged Mme. Meyers to get some help; we wanted to try to get to Switzerland. So she made contact with a butcher in Ponthion. He made a trip down towards an area of the Jura Mountains where he thought we could cross. However, he found it too well guarded and covered with too much snow. He recommended we go through the Pyrenees Mountains between Spain and France.

Wally and I couldn't believe it. Here we were in the northwest sector of France, and he was telling us the best way was through the Pyrenees all the way across to the southwest corner. But he insisted it would be the best way. They made contact with a gentleman in the town of Châlons, about forty miles away, who drove down in his automobile in the dark of night and took us to our next helpers.[2]

Andy Brenden and Wally Trinder climbed into the back seat of the car belonging to the gentleman from Châlons. It was late in the evening, and he drove at a steady pace, saying little, focusing on the road before him.

When they arrived in the city, he drove straight to a two-story house that sat back from the road with a lovely garden in front. He hastened to the door and knocked, then went back to get the two Americans. "This is where you will be staying for now. Go quickly inside," he said. Then he climbed back into his car and sped off.

Entering the house, Andy and Wally noticed that all the shutters were closed with only one small lamp lit in the hallway. A couple introduced themselves as Charles Perrin and his wife, Jacelyn. They spoke English fluently and inquired if the young men were hungry. Both replied "No thanks," and the Perrins then led them upstairs to a small bedroom.

The next morning, Andy and Wally had a chance to visit more extensively with their new helpers. "I'm an engineer in the ball bearing factory the Germans have taken over. But my loyalty is with Americans helping to fight against Germany," explained Charles. They turned out to be a lovely couple and very intelligent. Both evadees felt so much at home that they began to wish they could remain there for the duration of the war.

One evening after they had been with the Perrins several days, as they were finishing a supper of rabbit and Jacelyn was pouring tea, there was a sharp knock at the door. Charles opened it to find towering over him a Gestapo officer in his black uniform, red Nazi armband, and leather boots.

Jacelyn put her finger to her lips, signaling the American airmen to be silent and continue eating. They could hear the officer in the front hallway asking Charles in English if there were rooms available in the house that could be used for the German officers who were going to make their headquarters in Châlons. Wally and Andy glanced at each other, then at Jacelyn, who sat perfectly still, her eyes fixed on the front room. From where she sat, she couldn't see her husband or the officer but could hear everything that was happening just inside the foyer.

"I'm very sorry," said Charles, "but all the bedrooms are filled at the moment. I have friends staying with me from my college days. They will be leaving however in a few days, and then I will have rooms available."

"We need accommodations now," insisted the Gestapo officer. "We need them for our men. Let me see what you have."

"If you will wait here for just a moment, I will go up quickly to make sure it is presentable for you to go in. You can follow me," said Charles. He hurried upstairs and kicked the jackets belonging to the Americans under the bed.

As he turned around, the officer walked into the room, looked it over, and said, "This will be fine. We'll have this bedroom for our men." When he came back downstairs, Jacelyn met him in the hallway and pleaded with him. "Monsieur, if you please, it has been such a long time since we have had these visitors from school days. We will do everything in our power to make the officers comfortable when they do arrive. But, if they would only wait two days, we will have the room ready, and everything will be in perfect order for your men."

Mme. Perrin was an attractive woman with a gentle manner of speaking. The officer stared at her silently. Then he looked away for a moment and consented. As he walked past the large doorway leading into the dining room, he looked directly at Wally and Andy sitting at the table. The boys glanced up and looked back down at the table, pretending to be eating as casually as possible.

After a moment, the officer turned and left. Shutting the door and returning to his place at the head of the table, Charles picked up his cup of tea, but his hands were shaking so badly the liquid nearly sloshed out. Jacelyn came over and placed her arms gently on his shoulders. Charles grabbed her hand. No one said anything for several minutes. They all realized they had barely escaped a dangerous, even life-threatening, situation.

When Charles regained his composure, he told Wally and Andy that they would need to leave sooner than they had expected and instructed them to gather up their things immediately. Tomorrow he would drive them to a doctor's house—someone who might help them. But when they arrived early the next morning, the doctor wanted nothing to do with the American airmen. "My wife is expecting a child," he told them. "I am very sorry—I just don't want to take the chance."

He went on to explain that he knew two young women who owned a dress shop. One of them had previously worked in his household, and he trusted her completely. The women had said previously they would be willing to hide them for a couple of days if necessary. The three men climbed back into the car and drove to the shop. When they were inside, Charles said he needed to return home as quickly as possible. Andy and Wally thanked him profusely for all he and his wife had done for them and wished them the best. They hated for him to leave, but they knew there was no other option.

The women at the dress shop, Georgette and Andrea, were married, but their husbands were both in German slave camps. They kept up the pretense of a friendly relationship with several German soldiers who came and went from the shop, frequently bringing them candy and cigarettes. The shop owners passed these treats on to Andy and Wally, who often joked about thanking the Germans for the goodies.

Andy Brenden

Then one morning the girls gave us the news that we were going to a professor's house who was going to make plans for us to go to Paris. We were to make the trip by rail.

When we arrived at the professor's home, we stayed in the root cellar and were told it would be just a matter of a few days before we would leave. He told us we would have a guide to accompany us, someone who could speak English and who would show us the ropes and obtain tickets for us.

While we were there, the professor secured fake identification papers so we could have all the credentials necessary to travel through France. I went as Antoine Petit, an automobile mechanic. It was then we realized we were now dealing with someone who had deep connections with people working in a very organized way against the Germans. We were also given more authentic French clothing that made us look like real Frenchmen.

The day came when our young guide took us to the train station. He purchased three tickets and gave us ours. He said we would travel separately, never in a group, but to keep our eyes open for one another.

I was excited and nervous at the same time. It felt good to finally be on our way. But Wally and I both knew the dangers. We had shaken hands just before we got to the station. "Good luck, Wally. Say a prayer we make it okay," I said to him. We were on our way to Paris with the aid of the Underground. Our future seemed so uncertain. We were totally dependent on these Frenchmen who were risking everything for us.[3]

CHAPTER 16

A SQUEAKY WHEEL: GEORGE STARKS

The bicycling out of Chaumont was fairly easy...rolling countryside with the mountains still quite a distance ahead. Pump up the gentle hills and then just coast down the grades. More troop movements along the road of course, but it wasn't too bad.

I was about twelve kilometers on the other side of the town when I spotted two cyclists riding toward me from the south. They drew closer, and I could see that they were uniformed and armed Vichy police—no mistake about it.

As they rode past, I hung my head and tried to look unconcerned. I guess I appeared too unconcerned, for only seconds later one blew his shrill whistle for me to halt. I did—immediately.

Placing my foot on the pavement to steady my bike, I looked over my shoulder to see them pedaling back to me, pell-mell. When they reached me, they threw their bikes down, drew their pistols, and pointed the barrels to my head.

Of course these guys spoke French. They began to question me in quick, demanding tones and started to search me. I was caught.

"Je suis pilote américain. Parachute en France. Partais à Suisse." It was about the extent of what I could say in their language.

When I said that however, they both stepped back, looked at each [other], looked back at me, and began to converse between themselves. Soon they holstered their pistols.

They spoke to me in French and began to make gestures, pointing down the road from where they had just come from. I realized they were motioning me to be on my way. Then they began fingering their tunics and shaking their heads. They were warning me to stay away from anyone in a uniform like theirs.

I cannot fully understand to this day why they let me go. Perhaps even though their uniforms were Vichy, their hearts were French. Anyway, they went north, and I returned to cycling south.[1]

George continued down the road, heading away from Chaumont. The day was somewhat cloudy, and the cool temperatures made the bicycling more pleasant. He had only gone a short distance, however, when the front wheel began to squeak.

As he pedaled along, he realized the problem was the main axle. The bicycle was old, and the bearings were dry. The further he went the louder the squealing became. He began to worry that not only would the wheel fall apart, but that the noise would attract unwanted attention.

He continued riding until he reached a small hamlet with a few shops. He had planned not to stop but to ride straight through. The squealing had become so loud, however, that he had no choice. He hoped to find a mechanic or someone who could help him mend the bicycle. Fortunately, on the outskirts of the village, he spotted a repair garage and a man working on a car. He decided to take a chance and pedaled up to him. George got off the bike and pointed to the bearings. The mechanic looked quizzically at him for a moment. George wasn't sure what the man would do. But he turned and went back into the shadows of the shop and returned with an oil can. He gave the entire bike a generous oiling, and George told him, "Merci." He knew the mechanic recognized he wasn't French.

He climbed back on the bicycle and pedaled a short distance past the hamlet and back into the rolling countryside. In a field he saw a small deserted structure that looked like a barn. Taking a chance, he pedaled off the road, approached the dilapidated shack, and pushed open the door—it was empty.

"Guess this is as good a place as any to rest up and spend the night," he thought to himself, pushing his cycle into the barn. He found a corner in the shadows and sat down, his thoughts swirling. He wondered if his family had been notified and what had happened to his crew, but a deep sleep overcame him quickly. He was surprised to find the sun already breaking over the horizon when he awoke the next morning.

"How could I have slept that soundly?" he wondered and jumping up, immediately resumed his journey. The bicycle seemed wobbly, and he prayed it would hold up that morning. After riding for a while, he saw the large walled town of Langres ahead, built on a high promontory. George knew he didn't want to go through the town, and as he neared it he found that the road skirted the town along the high stone wall itself. Cycling around the town was tedious and tiring as the road took him up and down many hills. He thought how much he would have loved to visit Langres were he not so preoccupied with going unnoticed. He later learned it was an old Gallo-Roman fortress filled with artifacts and boasted a first-century gatehouse. But today was not the time for sightseeing.

No sooner had he started along the road that ran beside the wall than five German soldiers approached him on foot from the opposite direction and motioned for him to stop. George's hands started to tremble. As they came closer, he could hear them talking and made out the word "café." As they advanced toward him, his heart pounded. They said "café?" to him, thinking he was a local. He didn't make a sound and just pointed behind him to an entrance through the high wall into the town. Then he continued pedaling past them down the road. "They must have thought I was French, and they must not have known many words. Who cares?" he thought to himself. "It worked."

He was beginning to breathe a little easier as he turned the corner at the southern end of the walled area, where the road led into a long, arched tunnel. He had just entered when he realized there was a German roadblock in front of him. Coiled barbed wire stretched across the road with only a narrow opening in the middle, and a single young soldier stood there to check identification papers.

George didn't know what to do. He couldn't turn around. So he decided to climb off his bicycle and just keep going forward.

As he approached, the young German demanded "Papier! Papier!" He was asking George for identification. George just shrugged his shoulders and pointed back to the walled city as if to say, "I'm from there, and I'm too young to have papers." Then he made a split-second decision to turn his bicycle around and go back in the direction of the town. The young guard watched him but said nothing. George expected to get shot in the back at any moment.

Once back around the corner, the American got back on his bicycle and pedaled out into the countryside away from Langres with all its soldiers. He knew he had to circle around the town to stay away from soldiers, even if it meant rougher going. He began passing through a section of countryside with several small farmhouses dotting the hills in the distance, but he had no idea who might offer to help and who might turn him in.

The events of the day—three close calls—had left him completely drained, and he decided to push his bike out into the large, grassy field and hunker down behind one of the towering stacks of hay for the evening. Slumping to the grass, he sat with his back against the bale.

At this moment, the desperation of his situation seemed overpowering. It was so difficult being alone, not knowing who could be trusted.

Recalling the incident at the roadblock, he thought, "I should have been caught right then and there. I guess that German thought I was French and younger than sixteen, so not required to carry identification papers—but that guard was so young too. He had to have been a teenager himself. He was really green. If he had been an older soldier, I would have been caught for sure. Just one kid versus another kid in a war."

George wondered if his family had been notified that his plane had been shot down over German-occupied France. "Sure wish they knew I'm okay—for now anyway. I know they're worried." He thought about the pretty little majorette, Betty Jo, back in Florida. "She doesn't know if I'm dead or alive."

He laid his head back against the hay. "Wonder where my crew wound up? I pray they at least landed without too many injuries and that none of them got caught." His eyes were heavy, and he was tired to the bone. He said a quick prayer for his own safety before drifting off to sleep, but not soundly.

After tossing and turning most of the night, George got up at day-break. He had a few crackers in his sack, which he gulped down. He knew he had to get going again. He glanced over his silk map once more. "I guess I'll just keep heading south and see what happens."

As he rode along the terrain became increasingly difficult. Sometimes there was only a narrow, dirt mountain road to follow, sometimes a wagon trail or foot path. It now became apparent that he couldn't keep the bicycle. The front wheel was wobbling terribly, but the inclines made it nearly impossible to cycle. Deciding to abandon it, he pushed the bicycle over a slope into a thicket.

He continued to stay away from the main highway, taking a south-easterly road that went through Chassigny and Champlitte, down past Gray, and toward the city of Besançon. It was a long haul, and the hills were getting steeper as he neared the mountains that lay to the south. The Germans seemed to be everywhere in the Burgundian villages and towns, their trucks rumbling over the roads.

George's one great wish, to get in contact with someone who could help him get over the border into Switzerland—the Underground or the Resistance, maybe—seemed impossible. Hope was fading.

CHAPTER 17

LIFE IN STALAG LUFT III: IRV BAUM, TED BADDER, AND DALE BEERY

A chilly wind blowing from the north made the overcast day of March 25, 1944, even colder for newly captured American soldiers being processed as prisoners of war at Stamm-lager ("Stalag" for short) Luft III. Dozens of German officers stood about in small groups or paced back and forth along the edges of the dirt courtyard intently watching the proceedings conducted mostly by very young German soldiers.

There was a sense of high alertness everywhere in the camp. The guards were nasty, snapping at the new arrivals while staff cars filled with officers roared in and out of the gates. The Americans shuffled nervously in line awaiting their turn, quietly observing their new surroundings and occasionally making eye contact with one another. When it came time for Irv Baum to step forward to the wooden table, he was filled with overwhelming dread.

A seated German soldier pushed forward a simple form printed on pink paper with instructions to fill out the required information—name, rank, and serial number. When Irv finished writing his name, the German looked at the paper, then back up. "Put down religion also," he barked, staring at the new POW.

Irv felt anxious. His eye still had not healed from the blow he had received at capture, when his ethnicity surfaced. As he picked the pencil back up, the German turned around to answer someone who had called his name. Irv began to draw the straight line forming the first side of the letter "H" for "Hebrew." Suddenly he felt someone brush close against his side. A young German enlisted soldier discretely put his hand over the hand of the Jewish boy from New York, took away his pencil and hastily wrote "Protestant" on the form.

Irv was shocked when he realized what had happened. He looked directly into the clear blue eyes of the young man standing next to him, but his face was expressionless. The German then glanced away and signaled for Irv to move on.

The new POW didn't know what to make of it. Shaking his head, he began walking across the courtyard to his assigned barracks. "Well, what do you know? I guess some of them are okay," he thought, "just like we are." He would never forget the incident.

As he headed toward his wooden barracks, he caught a glimpse of Dale Beery, the substitute co-pilot who had been flying with them on their mission. About that time, Ted Badder crossed by near enough for Irv to call out to him quietly, "Hey, Ted, I think I just saw Beery, that guy who was our co-pilot in place of Willy. He must've been captured pretty quickly like we were."

"Really? I'll keep an eye out for him. Where are you going?" whispered Ted.

"Over there to that building, block 129, room 13—that barrack facing the fence in the South Compound, I think. Wonder what's up with all the tension? You can cut it with a knife," said Irv.

"Don't know. Take it easy, buddy," said Ted. "Maybe I'll see you soon. But so far so good. We've got pajamas and a toothbrush. Maybe we will even have clean sheets." Ted held up his cardboard suitcase.

A guard came over quickly, yelling at them not to talk anymore and to keep walking.

Both Americans had sensed the tension at Stalag Luft III from the time they arrived. When they entered their respective barracks, they found the other prisoners gathered in small groups excitedly talking in hushed tones. In the next couple of days, Irv and Ted found out why.

Located in the province of Lower Silesia (now part of Poland), about a hundred miles southeast of Berlin, Stalag Luft III was one of six POW camps operated by the Luftwaffe. It held several hundred men, and reciprocal agreements with Allied air forces about the treatment of POWs kept standards fairly high until the last stages of the war, when German defeat was imminent. Despite rules against visiting between compounds, communication among the prisoners was generally good, and they managed to exchange information about who had been captured.

The mix of POWs in Luft III included airmen from Britain and the Commonwealth, America, and other Allied nations. At first only officers were imprisoned there, but eventually non-commissioned prisoners arrived. The camp grew to more than sixty acres and housed about 2,500 Royal Air Force officers, seven thousand U.S. Army Air Force personnel, and some nine hundred officers from other Allied air forces, totaling nearly eleven thousand inmates.

During the first few days, both Ted and Irv were treated with suspicion, though they realized quickly that every new prisoner had to win the trust of his fellow inmates. Over the years several German spies pretending to be English or American had tried to infiltrate the barracks, though none was successful.

This camp was distinguished from all the others by two elaborate escape attempts. The first was known as the Wooden Horse. The second took place the day before Ted and Irv arrived. An escape of enormous proportions, it came to be known as the Great Escape.

"This place is all hyped up," Ted whispered to Irv when they crossed each other in the courtyard. They learned in the following days the incredible story of what had happened. After weeks of digging and preparing documents and clothes, seventy-seven troops—mostly RAF men—had crawled through one of the tunnels. Many more would have made it out had not a miscalculation in the length of the tunnel caused them to come up many yards short of their goal in the woods. Irv and Ted were enthralled by the tale. Though the POWs in charge wouldn't disclose many details, they heard enough to know what an incredible feat it had been.

Within a few weeks devastating news arrived at the camp. The prisoners' eager anticipation of any news of the escapees now turned to horror. They were sickened when the camp commander himself announced that of the seventy-seven who broke out of the camp, only three had gotten away, while fifty of the recaptured men had been shot by order of the Führer himself. Ted and Irv felt as let down as those who had been there longer and actually knew those courageous officers. It was devastating news, and for many days afterward a depressed mood hung over the entire camp.

Camp life developed a routine, and Ted and Irv saw each other a couple of times a week, usually somewhere in the courtyard. One day Ted noticed that Irv seemed distracted. "You okay?" Ted asked.

"Oh, there's some smart mouth in my barracks. Seems he doesn't like Jews," replied Irv. "He's been spouting off pretty good." Irv glanced up at his friend.

"Hey. Don't worry about it. What does he know?" said Ted, trying to console his friend, who still bore the scar from the German officer's blow when they were captured.

A few days later, when they were together again, Ted found Irv in a noticeably better mood. Before he could ask his friend how things were going in his barracks, Irv offered an explanation. "You know that guy I was telling you about—the one giving me trouble? Well, a couple of the other guys took care of him—told him he'd have to stop it or there'd be consequences. Then one of the senior officers got him moved to another barrack. Don't know how they did it but they did," said Irv, grinning.

Ted was glad for his buddy. Most importantly, the Germans didn't get wind of it, and Irv remained thankful for the young German soldier who had signed him into Stalag Luft III as Protestant.

Many of the officers imprisoned at Stalag Luft III had already established their reputations in their chosen fields before the war. Others became well-known afterward as leaders in education, politics, theater, or music. Irv knew some of these men personally, while others, because of the restrictions on fraternizing, he only heard about. Even within the same compound, it was often difficult to continue relationships with someone living in a different barrack.

One man in particular made a deep impression on Irv—and in a most unexpected way. His name was Murdo Ewen Macdonald, called Padre Mac by those who knew him.[1]

Born in 1914 on the Isle of Harris in the most mountainous part of the Outer Hebrides of Scotland, Macdonald progressed from humble origins to St. Andrew's University, where he became the Scottish universities' middleweight boxing champion. His chief interest, however, was religion, and by 1940, when he was commissioned as a chaplain to the Queen's Own Cameron Highlanders, he was considered one of Scotland's greatest preachers.

He also had a reputation for being courageous and defiant, even in the face of death. In 1942, he joined the First Parachute Brigade. Severely wounded on a mission in North Africa, he was taken captive by the Germans. Rumor had it that he blew up the German plane that had brought him to Italy, but the Germans were reluctant to execute him because of his fame as a minister. Incarcerated at Stalag Luft III, Macdonald became involved with the Great Escape, transporting sand dug from the tunnel to the yards or wherever he could deposit it undetected.

True to his calling, Padre Mac began holding church services every Sunday and quickly gained a reputation within Luft III as a speaker and counselor. For his untiring ministry to the American POWs, the United States conferred on him the Bronze Star after the war.

Hearing other servicemen speak of Padre Mac's oratorical skill, the young Jew from the Catskills decided to attend his service one Sunday morning. "Nothing else to do," remembers Irv. Macdonald's impressive ability to convey the hope of his faith had its effect. Baum attended his services regularly, as did hundreds of other young men. "He would start very soft and almost slow, then build throughout his sermon. I really loved to listen to him," says Baum. "He helped fill a spiritual void for me—he did the same for Badder—it really changed Ted."

CHAPTER 18

11, RUE DE SAUSSAIES, GESTAPO HEADQUARTERS, PARIS: DICK MORSE

W hen the four Germans captured me and my buddy, they frisked us but didn't treat us roughly. One of them said, "English?" and I answered, "No, American." Then they took us to a small car, a Fiat, I believe, and two of them sat on the back seat, then Joe and I had to crawl in on top of them. So there were six of us in that tiny car.

They drove the short distance to Cognac, marched us across the street and into a large building similar to a city hall, up the stairs, and into a sparsely furnished room where an English-speaking man was sitting at a desk, and he told us to sit down.

As the German soldiers were leaving, one spied my wristwatch, had it half off my hand, then hesitating, pushed it back in place on my wrist. This watch was given to me by my parents when I graduated from high school. My mother passed away a couple of years later and this watch was very important to me. I was glad he had second thoughts and allowed me to keep it.

The man at the desk asked if were hungry. We said "Yes," so he took us downstairs to a large dining room where about fifty German soldiers were eating. We were seated on a platform where there was a table and two chairs. We could see the soldiers watching and talking about us.

A young lady was waiting on the tables. I recognized her as the girl wearing the green scarf, whom we had seen at the farm. I suddenly wondered if she had been the one who had turned us in.

She brought us a plate of stew, and it was delicious. When she returned she said, "Encore, encore?" and one of the soldiers nearby said, "She wants to know if you want more."

Joe and I both said, "Yes." We were really hungry.

That was the last good meal we had until later in September.[1]

Guards escorted both Americans to a small French jail just up the street from the municipal building and placed them in separate cells. It was still light outside, and Dick gazed out the window. Almost immediately two young children came up, pushing two apples and some cherries through the bars. He tried to converse with the youngsters, but neither spoke English. They did make out the word "airplane," because they used their hands to mimic flying. There was a set of bunk beds in his cell, so he climbed into the upper bunk. The hot meal topped off by apples and cherries made a difference in how he felt. He reflected back to the waitress.

"I guess she may have been the one who turned us in—she must've gotten scared," he thought to himself. He remembered the people who had already risked their lives for him. "If it was her, I don't hold it against her," he thought, as he drifted off to sleep.

In the middle of the night, Dick suddenly awoke when he heard his cell door rattling open. A French guard came in with a bottle of cognac and offered it. Dick thanked him but refused.

He insisted in broken English, so Dick took the bottle and had a small swallow. It reminded him of the time he had breakfast with

Maurice Collette, when his mother had prepared eggs for him on his first morning in France after the crash. He would never forget the sting—and surprise—of that big gulp of cognac.

Joe told Dick the following day that a bottle of cognac had been passed to him also through the small window in his cell door. Joe said he was so certain they would be killed that he drank the entire contents.

The next morning, after the two prisoners were given a small breakfast of bread and coffee, German guards loaded them into the back of a truck and drove forty miles to a civilian jail in Angoulême.

When they arrived, Dick and Joe were taken into a small office, where a smiling German guard told them in perfect English, "For you, the war is over." He directed them to put all of their possessions on the counter—identification bracelets, pencils, and the contents of their escape kits with map, money, and compass.

Dick watched as the guard placed the contents into a manila envelope, sealed it, and had them write their names and home addresses on it. They were assured that when the war was over these things would be returned, and in fact, Dick received his envelope several months after the war ended.

The Germans confined Dick and Joe here for three days until, at about seven o'clock in the morning, they were handcuffed together and escorted to the train by two soldiers. "Well, it looks like they are taking us to Paris," said Dick to his nervous friend. "What's going to happen next?" Around midnight they arrived in Paris, where a car awaited the group. Dick and Joe remained handcuffed to each other and to a blanket rail inside the car.

The vehicle drove up the Champs-Élysées and around the Arc de Triomphe and stopped at 11, rue de Saussaies—Gestapo headquarters.[2] The prisoners were marched upstairs to a nearly empty room. They were handcuffed to chairs across a table from a man who never spoke but continued studying papers on his desk, occasionally making notes and writing comments.

It was now two or three o'clock in the morning, and the man pulled out a sandwich to eat. He continued working busily at whatever was occupying all his attention. Once or twice his head would begin to nod, but then he would jerk awake again and return to his task.

Joe looked around anxiously. Dick tried to sleep a little, but his adrenaline kept him awake. They would glance at each other wondering what would happen to them next. They knew they were in the hands of the Gestapo, notorious for torture and executions. Having been captured in civilian clothes, they could be shot as spies. And many people had helped them—many people whom they did not wish to betray.

CHAPTER 19

FRESNES PRISON, PARIS: DICK MORSE CONT'D

The following morning, May 30, 1944, as it began to get light, Joe and I found ourselves still handcuffed to our chairs. I looked out a nearby window and in the early morning mist could see the top of the Eiffel Tower in the distance. It was a surreal sight. I had no idea I would see it—or for that matter ever be in Paris—when we left on our bombing mission back on March 16.

Evidently the man had worked all through the night on his paperwork—except of course for the moments he had dozed off. He looked haggard but, amazingly, continued to work on.

Suddenly several soldiers came in, unhooked us from the chairs, and took us outside to another car. After traveling about thirty minutes or so, we stopped at a huge stone prison, which looked cold and ominous. It turned out to be the infamous civilian prison Fresnes, built in the late 1800s.

*We were taken inside to a very large room surrounded by three tiers
of cells. Joe and I were placed into one on the lower floor. As we sat on
our bunks, two cigarettes and matches were slid under the door.*

*Later that day, my buddy and I were separated. I was placed in a
cell about ten feet across and about twelve feet deep. It contained a sink,
toilet, and bunk. There was a very high barred, six-foot window in one
corner with opaque panes, except for one in the upper corner. By standing on the sill, I could see the sky.*

*It's funny how much more appealing the sky appears when you are
a prisoner of war.*[1]

Constructed between 1895 and 1898, Fresnes Prison was at the time
of World War II the largest penal institution in France. Located just south
of Paris, it was built in what became known as the "telephone pole"
design, with cells extending crosswise from a central corridor. The enormous fieldstone structure could hold more than 1,500 prisoners in single-
cell confinement. Under Nazi occupation, the prison held captured
British spies and members of the French Resistance and Underground.
Torture and execution were part of daily existence here for many inmates.
The Allied advance on Paris in the summer of 1944 proved fatal for those
still incarcerated at Fresnes. On August 25, just days before the liberation
of the capital, the Gestapo killed most of the remaining prisoners.

Two days after Dick arrived at Fresnes, two more prisoners were
shoved into his cell. One, a Canadian major, Jim Hill, was as mad as hell
at having been captured. A Spitfire pilot in the Royal Air Force, he
wanted to keep flying to defeat the Germans. The other was a B-17
bombardier named Charlie Bond from Alabama. Since there was only
one bunk in the cell, Dick yielded it to the higher-ranking Hill and slept
on the floor along with Charlie.

The prison was filthy. Decades of dirt and grime caked the interior
surfaces, and the stale air reeked of urine. But Dick was glad to have the

company of the other two airmen. He regretted not being able to see or talk to his buddy Joe, however, and hoped he was all right.

The next morning guards brought them a breakfast of ersatz coffee and two or three slices of dark bread, which was made with sawdust. Although it was filling, it had little nutrition. At noon they were given a bowl of watery soup, ersatz coffee, and two slices of dark bread. At night it was the same meal. Occasionally there might be small pieces of potato or turnip, and once in a while small shreds of some kind of meat.

The soup was served from a huge kettle on a cart, pushed along the corridor in front of their cells on a track carved out in the concrete floor. Turnkeys passed meals to prisoners through small windows in the cell doors. Every other week or so, a woman came by with a rack of books, and the prisoners were allowed to choose something to read.

But often interrogations were the order of the day. The interrogators were usually quite skilled and often used force to get what they wanted. On several occasions Dick felt intense pressure but never gave up anything more than his name, rank, and serial number. He guessed that since he was a low-ranking noncommissioned officer, his captors assumed he had little useful information. He was certainly thankful, because he often heard moans and muffled screams coming from the interrogation rooms.

One day in early August, the guards took Dick and about twenty other Americans to a large room, where he was delighted to find his old buddy Joe in the group. They immediately reconnected with one another. As they caught up with each other's news, a doctor entered the room. He checked everyone for fleas and lice. Again Dick and Joe were fortunate to show only minor signs of infestation. Another GI was so badly bitten that he was returned to his cell.

After the exams the prisoners were handcuffed in pairs and loaded into trucks. Soon the group under heavy guard reached the station and transferred to a waiting train. Eight prisoners were deposited into each compartment, along with several guards.

When one of the guards passed Dick, he asked where they were going. "You are very fortunate—you go to the Fatherland," he threw his head back and laughed at his prisoner.

Dick Morse

Joe and I were in the same car, but he was handcuffed to another prisoner, and they were sitting near a window. I believe his partner's name was Childs, and he was a navigator from Colorado. We were given some buttered bread, and he asked Joe to scrape the butter off his bread and give it to him so he could put it on his wrist and slip out of the handcuffs.

There were several drunk German soldiers on the train, and our guards were members of the Gestapo. It was a warm day and the windows were partly open.

As it began to get dark, we approached the German border when suddenly Childs, who had been able to free his hand from the cuffs, jumped out the window of the moving train. Immediately guards signaled for the train to stop. The Gestapo and all the drunken solders rushed in and started hitting anyone they could reach. Then they really lit into Joe and told him he was going to be sorry. They searched the area but didn't find Childs, and we never heard what happened to him.

The train started back up, and I hated thinking about actually heading into Germany. Our situation seemed to get more helpless with each passing hour.[2]

CHAPTER 20

DULAG LUFT AND THE FORTY-AND-EIGHTS: DICK MORSE CONT'D

he train carrying Dick and the other prisoners rumbled further into Germany, finally stopping in Wiesbaden. The guards herded all their prisoners, still cuffed in pairs, out to waiting trucks and transported them to yet another civilian prison.

Dick was now tired to the bone, exhausted from the trip and struggling under the weight of anxiety. As before, he was placed in solitary confinement. From what he could determine, so were the twenty other American prisoners. He lay down on his bunk, wondering how his buddy Joe was.

After about three days, Dick was led handcuffed to another three-story structure down the street, apparently an old municipal building, and led into a small, sparsely furnished office, where a Gestapo officer sat behind a large desk. The prisoner was told to sit down on a chair in front of him. In short, terse phrases, the interrogator asked questions about the group and squadron he was with when shot down, the date of his shoot-down, and the names of his crew members.

Dick proceeded to say, as he had done previously during interrogations, that according to the Geneva Conventions he was required to provide only his name, rank, and serial number. This seemed to frustrate his interrogator. "You were in civilian clothes when you were captured," barked the German. "I want the names of those who helped you. You are either a spy, saboteur, or terrorist."

Dick pulled his dog tags out and placed them on the desk in front of him. The interrogator picked them up and threw them across the room. "Anybody can get these," he yelled. "Let me make myself clear. If you do not cooperate with us, you can be executed. I will let you think about this for now. But your meals will be cut in half. Get him out of here." The guard who had escorted Dick to the building motioned with his rifle to get up. The session was over for the day.

Dick went back to his cell. He had not had a good meal since he left Cognac. When the civilian who was responsible for serving his thin soup that night appeared at his cell door, the guard told him not to dip too far down in the liquid where most of the solid pieces of food were. As a result, Dick had only a cupful of thin liquid. Though he was in the civilian prison in Wiesbaden for only about six weeks, he lost nearly twenty-five pounds there. Each time he was interrogated he refused to give more information than name, rank, and serial number, and each time his rations were reduced further.

The bombings by the Allies continued. Because the prison was close to a train station, prisoners could hear the explosions. When sirens sounded, the guards would hurry into the basement, leaving prisoners locked in their cells. Occasionally the bombs fell so close that POWs could smell the cordite and see smoke billowing outside their cell windows. When it was over, the alarm would sound again, and guards would return to their duties.

One afternoon as Dick was sitting on his bunk, his cell door banged open. In walked a high-ranking German officer in a uniform covered with decorations. In training, young American airmen had been taught to show respect for officers, even if they were the enemy.

Dick came to attention and the officer just stood there staring at the young airman for several minutes. Then, without saying a word, he turned around and walked back out. The American never knew why he had come to his cell and later, when asking around, never found anyone else who had had such an experience.

Eventually, the several dozen prisoners were moved from the prison in Wiesbaden and loaded on a train bound for a Dulag Luft, an indoctrination and processing center outside of Frankfurt.

Dick Morse

We were being taken deeper into Germany. We all knew that. When we arrived in Frankfurt, we were made to walk quite a distance to a Dulag Luft, where we were interrogated once more, received different clothing, and finally got some food, though not much.

I was given a used British uniform, some black shoes, and an overcoat. Then I was put into a small, white room with a very large, bright light and was kept there for the rest of the day.

About two days later, fifty or sixty of us were taken to a train station and crowded into what was called a "Forty and eight" boxcar. These train cars were built during the First World War to carry either forty men or eight horses. Evidently the Germans had used them to carry horses and livestock, because they were extremely dirty and smelly. In each car was one small, high window up in the corner. That's all the air circulation we had.

Railroads were targets for bombing and strafing, and these trains had no markings on them for identification. The Allies had no way of knowing the trains were carrying helpless POWs.

We traveled about a day and arrived at a large, barn-like building in St. Wendel, Germany. There were about four hundred prisoners on the train, and we stayed there nearly two weeks.

Then in September, once again we were crowded into boxcars. These boxcars were divided with wire fencing into two sections for prisoners, with a smaller section in the middle for the guards. Our section was so crowded that we could not all sit down at one time but had to take turns.

In the center of our section there was a can that we used for a toilet and occasionally, it spilled all over the floor.

One day as I was sitting near the wire barrier, I saw a German coin that apparently had been dropped by one of the guards, and when I got a chance I reached through the wire and picked it up. I still have it.[1]

CHAPTER 21

STALAG LUFT IV, DEEPER INTO GERMANY: DICK MORSE CONT'D

W e arrived in Berlin late in the night and stayed for a few hours but were not allowed to leave our section. Finally, after four more days of traveling, we reached the prison camp in Keifheide, in the Pomeranian Forest in eastern Prussia, near the Baltic Sea. The area is now part of Poland.

When we debarked the train, we marched two or three miles to Stalag Luft IV,[1] where we were separated into groups. There were almost ten thousand interred there, and most of them were American Air Force non-commissioned officers and some Royal Air Force non-commissioned officers. Because all the barracks were full, we were put into small huts large enough for ten people, but twenty were put into each. We stayed there for about two weeks while a new compound was being completed.

The camp was set in a forest clearing about one and a half miles square, and it was surrounded by dense forests. There were two barbed *wire fences ten feet high completely surrounding it. The outer fence was electrically charged. Between the two fences was another fence of rolled barbed wire four feet high. There was an area about two hundred feet wide between the fence and the edge of the forest, so anyone attempting to escape would be in full view of the tower guards who had powerful spotlights and many machine guns.*

There were four sections—A, B, C, and D—with ten barracks each, and each barrack held about two hundred prisoners, eighteen to a room. Joe and I were put in Section C, Barrack 8, Room 7. The only furniture was one six-foot table and a bench, and there were no bunks, but excelsior had been spread on the floor for us to sit and sleep on.

The only running water available was cold water from one faucet and no flushing toilets—only a small covered building outside with ten holes, lined up in a row, which we could use during the day. No one was allowed outside after dark, so there was a latrine with two holes at the end of the barrack for about 240 POWs to use at night.

These latrines were cleaned out occasionally by Russian POWs and the contents spread on the fields outside the camp area. Outside of each lager there were two wells with pumps to provide washing and drinking water, but not facilities for bathing, and although there were fleas, lice, bedbugs, and parasites, no means for delousing.

Our building was roughly built of wooden slabs covered with tar paper and was on posts about three feet off the ground. There was no insulation and very little heat—only a small stove in one corner.

Each day we were given six or seven pieces of fuel that resembled coal, which we could use to make a fire. During the day we could go outside and move around, but the evenings were long and colder, and there was little to do. Because we had to sit and sleep on the cold floor, we saved our fuel to use then. We did not undress but slept in our clothes, even our overcoats, and we each had one blanket, so Joe and I slept together. We were warmer sharing our two blankets.[2]

Life at the Camp

At about five or six in the morning, the guards would come in shouting "Raus mit!"—"Out with you!"—and we had to go outside, line up, and be counted. There were about two hundred in each barrack, and at times it would be snowy, windy, and way below zero. If the count didn't come out right, it was redone until everyone was accounted for.

When we returned inside, one fellow from each room would take a pail and go to the "kitchen" to get the breakfast, which consisted of ersatz [coffee] and several loaves of sawdust bread, which would be divided between those in the room. We each had a cup, bowl, fork, and spoon. The noon and evening meals consisted of sawdust bread and thin watery soup.

The Geneva Conventions stated we could not be required to work, and we were supposed to eat as well as the men guarding us, but I'm not sure we did. There was very little meat—occasionally bits and pieces in the watery soup and no milk or greens. The food we were given had very little nourishment. A Physician Review states that they have come to the conclusion that actual caloric values given by the Germans were camouflaged to starve prisoners to death, and it was planned and officially approved.

Calorie deficiency caused plagues of contagious diseases such as diarrhea, dysentery, diphtheria, tuberculosis, and pneumonia, and often led to death. The German bread consisted of 50 percent bruised rye grain, 20 percent sliced sugar beets, 20 percent sawdust, and 10 percent minced leaves or straw. Although the bread was claimed officially to have 674 calories, in reality it had only 314.

Once in a while we received Red Cross packages containing food prepared for one person, but they had to be divided between several. It was said that the guards often kept them for themselves. If there were canned foods in these packages, the guards would puncture them so we had to eat them right away and not stash them away with us if we planned to escape.

During the day we could go outside, and we would walk around the yard. No more than two prisoners could talk together, or a guard had to be with them. Before dark, around four p.m., we had to go inside and the shutters were closed for the night. There wasn't much to do, and we all had body lice, which were not only itchy but also carried typhus fever, so we spent a lot of time picking them off our clothes. During the night, we would hear guards with their dogs patrolling under our building.[3]

CHAPTER 22

ANGELS WATCHING OVER: DON EDGERLY, BOB WILLIAMS, BILL WYATT

The three crewmen continued on walking in a southeasterly direction toward Switzerland. Perhaps three of them looked less suspicious than a lone traveler would have. In any case, they encountered no major problems, and they were grateful to have each other to talk to and for encouragement. Only when they were going through small villages did they not speak, to keep from drawing attention.

Bill Wyatt

Most of the French people were wonderful to us, giving us food, clothes, and a place to sleep. Everyone hated the Germans and was only too glad to help us. Three different times we were able to stay at a farmhouse and rest up after we left the Lamberts, but only for a day at a time—nevertheless, we did appreciate it. Several times we came across Germans, but nothing happened.

We kept walking using our compasses, always heading southeast. In survival we had been told that if there was any way to get across into Switzerland, that would be the best route to take.

Only when we were thirteen kilometers from the Swiss frontier did we meet the French Underground. We were coming into a small village early one morning and stopped at the window of a bakery. The bread looked so good, and we were starving. It must have been the owner who opened the door and just looked at us for a moment.

Bob looked at her, and I guess he was just tired and out of options. He told her we were Americans. She quickly motioned us into her shop and told us to wait there. She went into the back and in a few minutes came back out followed by a young man.

In broken English he told us to follow him. He would take us to someone who could help us. And sure enough, he took us to an older man who was with the Resistance. He said he would lead us over the Alps through a pass he knew about. We couldn't believe our luck. We both said to each other later that angels were looking after us that day.

We did have one really scary incident. After our guide took us through a pass and pointed us to cross over an open field, he said his good-byes. We were about halfway across when a soldier came out of nowhere with his guard dog and yelled for us to halt. I thought for sure he was German and that we were caught and about to be POWs.

But when he came up to us, it turned out he was part of a Swiss patrol—their uniforms resembled German uniforms—that's why [there was] the confusion. We were actually already in Switzerland and didn't know it. We couldn't believe it. It would have been really difficult to cross over without the help of the man who guided us, because there were guards everywhere, and you had to know exactly where to cross. We were just fortunate, that's all.[1]

CHAPTER 23

TROOP TRAIN AND A BRAVE MAN: ANDY BRENDEN AND WALLY TRINDER

The trip to Paris was really rough. Wally and I found a couple of empty seats, but the train rocked back and forth along the tracks. We kept an eye on one another from a distance.

Finally we arrived at the Paris railroad station. We were to make connections immediately to travel on to Toulouse, a city in southern France.

But when we arrived in Paris, we found that the train we wanted to take was being delayed for some reason. We walked out onto the platform, and our guide came up to us and instructed us to board a troop train that was also going south. He said to jump on it at the very last minute and to make ourselves as inconspicuous as possible.

It was about nine p.m. when the train started pulling out. We jumped aboard along with quite a number of others who couldn't make the regular passenger cars.

When we were aboard, we stood in the aisle rather than going into the individual compartments. The German soldiers were walking by, a steady stream of them, brushing against us and stepping on our toes. We were quite uncomfortable.[1]

The troop train carrying Andy and Wally was only about thirty minutes outside of Paris when airplanes began bombing the depot and demolishing the tracks behind them. The bombs also ripped up several sections of track in front of the train, forcing it to halt.

The entire train emptied, and its passengers frantically searched for cover. Wally and Andy ran for a ditch and wound up not far from one another, lying on their stomachs to avoid flying debris.

As soon as the planes flew off, crews began working to mend enough track to allow the train to continue. The repairs were completed by about midnight, and the train was on its way again.

After re-boarding, Andy was standing near the bathroom. The train had not been traveling long when a German soldier came up to him and asked him to hold his gun while he used the toilet. Andy had no idea what he was saying, but the soldier simply thrust his rifle into Andy's hands and turned to enter the small compartment.

"Brother," Andy thought to himself, "I'm really in trouble now." But when the soldier emerged from the bathroom, he grabbed his rifle out of Andy's hand and went on his way. "He's probably just some ordinary guy like I am," thought Andy. It was the Gestapo and SS troops that the American evaders knew they needed to watch out for.

As the train neared Toulouse, the guide came up and whispered that everyone's identification papers were being inspected. When the train stopped people began walking around in the cars, and Andy thought he saw someone pointing to Wally. He motioned for Wally to come with him to one of the restrooms. Inside they found several duffel bags stowed there to make room for more passengers in the cars. Pushing the bags against the door, the airmen stood still, their hearts pounding.

"We're going to be in trouble," whispered Andy to Wally. They decided to try to stay hidden in the bathroom during the inspection. Momentarily, they could hear the inspector pushing against the door trying to open it. Andy stared at Wally. The inspector was able to push it open just slightly, looked down, saw the duffel bags, and made no further attempt to get in. Once the train started back up, the two servicemen pushed the bags away from the door and re-entered the hallway.

About twenty minutes from Toulouse, the civilians in the compartment where Andy and Wally were standing began whispering back and forth and looking toward the Americans, but nothing seemed to happen. As soon as the train stopped, they both rushed out and separated into the crowd. They had no idea where their guide was. Andy kept Wally in his sight, and finally the guide came up behind him and then passed on in front, a signal to follow. Wally saw the two of them and followed.

As the guide began walking up a ramp leading out of the depot, Andy became aware of a large man, well over six feet tall, following him at a distance of some forty or fifty feet. Once outside the depot, the guide continued walking into Toulouse, eventually stopping at a café and motioning for the two young men to sit down at the table with him. He ordered beer for all three. Soon the large man Andy had noticed following him walked by. The guide nodded toward him, and the two Americans realized they were supposed to follow him.

Close by sat two German soldiers laughing and drinking their beer, so there was no way to thank this young guide for all his help. Andy and Wally stood up and looked at him, hoping he recognized how much they appreciated what he had done for them. They both knew they were unlikely to cross paths with him again.

The large man continued walking into a densely populated part of the city, finally stopping at a residence with a door that opened directly onto the street. Above the door was a sign that read "Employment Service." The man pushed open the door and stood inside to allow the Americans to enter. Once inside he locked the door and led them down a narrow corridor to a back room. Andy realized that the big Frenchman walked with a slight limp, and found out later that he had a wooden leg.

"I'm M. Collaire," said the big man, shaking hands with each airman. They didn't realize it, but their journey had brought them to the very doorstep of the leader of the Underground in southern France.

They stayed with Collaire for several days, during which time he helped other refugees, including Polish and English evaders all seeking instructions for traveling to Spain. Andy and Wally found him to be one of the most remarkable people they had ever met.

A few days later, on May 1, they watched from a second story window as Collaire walked along the streets below singing patriotic songs with other French citizens. May Day had been a national holiday celebrating workers' rights, but under German occupation, the French were not allowed to celebrate. Nevertheless, singing had broken out spontaneously, and Collaire was participating with gusto.

Suddenly two younger German soldiers came up and told him to be quiet—no singing was allowed. When they pulled out their pistols, the feisty Frenchman slapped the weapons out of their hands and continued to sing. The stunned soldiers simply backed off and allowed the robust man to continue his songs.

A few days later, Collaire looked up from breakfast and said to Andy and Wally, "Come on. I'm going to show you the German planes and their repair depot." The two young men stared back at him hardly knowing what to say.

"Sir," said Andy, "pardon me, but we don't care one thing about seeing any German planes or depots."

"Right," chimed in Wally, "we're just fine staying right here."

He laughed at them and said, "Don't worry. I'll take care of everything."

Reluctantly, the boys followed Collaire to his car. He drove a short distance out of town to a large field. At the gate the guard stopped the car and asked for identification.

"I don't need identification. I'm loyal to the Germans. They know me. Let me through and don't bother me," he told the flabbergasted guard. And with that, he pressed down on the accelerator and drove past the gate. When they reached the airfield, he drove all around the airplanes, and Andy and Wally were able to see a few Fw 190s and other German planes up close. After showing them everything on the German base, Collaire drove back to his house without incident.[2]

Andy Brenden

When he said he was going to take us to that German base, Wally and I just couldn't believe our ears. We were scared to death the entire time.

But M. Collaire was a gentleman we came to have a great amount of respect for: he had tremendous courage and went about his activities helping people evade and escape without any regard for his own safety.

While we lived in his home, we always had evenings full of entertainment with him. He could speak a little English, and he was teaching us French. We would play checkers with him, games full of friendly competition and laughter.

But the time had come when we would leave Toulouse to begin making our way to the Pyrenees Mountains and then walk across them. He told us he would make all the arrangements.

The evening before we were to leave, his wife baked us a cake and decorated it with American flags. We had a party that evening with all those who would be leaving when Wally and I left.

As before, we hated to be on our way. We felt safe there—at least as safe as we could be in the midst of war and survival. But we were closer than ever to what we hoped would be our final push to freedom.[3]

CHAPTER 24

THE CAPTAIN: ANDY BRENDEN AND WALLY TRINDER CONT'D

M. Collaire drove Wally and Andy a short distance beyond Toulouse and stopped at a deserted country crossroads. Soon a vehicle arrived, and the driver was introduced to the airmen only as the "captain."

He pointed to the back of his truck, which was filled with oats, and in heavily accented English told the boys to get in. The captain covered them with the grain, spoke briefly with Collaire, and sped away with his hidden "packages." After a long and bumpy drive—Wally and Andy guessed the captain was using back roads—he stopped and dug through the oats, helping the airmen out of their hiding place.

Brushing off their clothes, Wally and Andy realized they were on a farm with a cottage next to a pen filled with a few sheep and goats. "Hey, look there," said Andy to Wally, who was still trying to get oats out of his shoes. Wally turned around to see the Pyrenees Mountains rising behind them. "Wow," said Wally, shaking his head. It was the first time since their shoot-down that they thought they really might escape from German-occupied France.

"Come on. Let's get inside," said their new patron, and they followed him inside the farmhouse. He busied himself with making supper for the three of them, a simple meal of stew with some bread, a little cheese, and wine.

The captain was an elderly gentleman—Andy wondered just how old he might be. His full grey beard and mustache made it more difficult to guess. When he took off his jacket however, Andy could see that whatever his age, he was very muscular with large biceps and forearms, obviously accustomed to hard physical labor. He moved briskly around the small kitchen area and soon had their meal ready.

As the three men sat down together, the captain paused momentarily to say grace over the meal. When he looked up, he began talking animatedly to the airmen about how they needed to get in shape physically to walk over the Pyrenees. "We start in the morning," he said gruffly but with a twinkle in his eye. "I get you in shape!"

The following day, true to his word, the captain placed an axe in Andy's hand and pointed to a large pile of wood that needed to be chopped for firewood. Wally was given the task of feeding the sheep and goats and moving them from one pasture to another. Later the captain marked out a course up and down the hills at the back of his farm for the airmen to run. Neither of them had any trouble sleeping at night.

During the evenings their host pulled out a set of checkers, a game at which he almost always got the best of them. During one of the games, he said they needed to award the winner a prize. Laughing heartily, he said, "For every time I win, I can pull a hair from your head and every time I lose, you can pull one out of my goatee!"

Andy and Wally frequently questioned him about what was going to happen next and how they were going to make the journey. "Mind your own judgment," the captain responded. "You are with an organized movement now. Everything will be taken care of. All you do is follow instructions, listen, and do no talking."

After Andy and Wally had been with the captain for nearly a week, they were sitting at the kitchen table when there was a rap at the door. A robust man, tall and lean, entered and began speaking perfect English. He greeted the captain with a firm handshake, and it was clear they were old and trusted friends. The visitor introduced himself as Frisco and asked to speak to the two Americans separately.[1]

CHAPTER 25

"FRISCO": ANDY BRENDEN AND WALLY TRINDER CONT'D

Andy Brenden

I think his real name was Joe Bairre, or something like that, but he told me and Wally to just call him Frisco. It turned out that he could speak such incredible English because he was an American!

He had come to France and married a French girl and did not return to the United States as instructed. He must have had a little trouble with the State Department.

But his wife and two children had been killed by the Germans, and he was on the loose and angry. He was a wild, wild man, trying in some way to get even with the Germans. I guess he felt that helping the Americans across the Pyrenees Mountains might in some way justify the mistake he made to his country.

He begged us to go to whatever authority we could to try and justify his error, and we promised him we would do whatever we could if we got back.[1]

Frisco began planning the trip across the Pyrenees in earnest. The following day he brought to the farmhouse two more men who planned to cross and indicated there would be others as well. These other men were not Americans but members of the Underground, facing certain torture and execution if they were captured. It became clear to Andy and Wally that this man Frisco had done this many times and knew exactly what to do.

The next afternoon around four o'clock he arrived at the farmhouse and directed the two Americans to come with him in his car. Andy and Wally shook hands with the elderly captain, who laughed and told them he would miss pulling out their hairs, a reference to all the times he had bettered them at checkers.

Frisco drove for a while and reached a cemetery. After he had driven in among the tombstones, he instructed them to lie low behind the large grave markers, keeping out of sight. He would return shortly with the others who were to make the trip with them.

Andy felt nervously excited: this would be the last part of their long journey. He prayed everything would go smoothly. Wally was behind a tombstone not far away from him, and they signaled to one another with a discreet wave. They both knew the time had come.

Andy heard the crunch of gravel as a car entered the cemetery. He peeked over the top of the marker. It was Frisco with another group of travelers. One more round trip—a total of eight men were now hiding among the tombstones.

Shortly before midnight, the robust American working diligently with the French Underground returned, dressed in clothes that reminded Andy of a Robin Hood costume. Wally asked him where in the world he had gotten clothes like that. "Well," said Frisco, "there was a German lying up there in the hills, and I needed this outfit worse than he did. Of course I had to shoot him to get it. If I can get anything more from German soldiers to add to my collection, I'll be happy to do that too."

He quickly rounded up the others, and together they began walking toward the mountains. Since the immediate area was level ground, he hoped to get into the hills before sunrise. Nevertheless, the group did not make as much progress as Frisco hoped. At dawn, as they were about to cross one of the last roads before arriving at the foothills, a large contingent of German motorcycles suddenly could be heard around the bend in the road, headed their way.

Frisco motioned for everyone to scatter and hide. Andy and Wally had just enough time to dive into some bushes before the soldiers sped past. They lay quietly for several minutes until Frisco could be heard giving a sharp whistle, the sign to join him quickly again. Continuing, they soon reached a wooded area in the hills, and their guide decided they should all lie low until evening. They spread out some, but Andy and Wally sat together against a tree. Andy looked down at his hiking boots. "Hey, man, I sure am glad we have these," he said.

"Yeah," said Wally. Both men had been given hiking boots by the captain. He had explained that these would be much more comfortable than what they were wearing—worn leather lace-ups—to hike up and down the hills and mountains.

That night Frisco led them further into the hills, but since it was nighttime, the traveling was slower and becoming more difficult. Early in the morning he allowed them to sleep, then continued on at daybreak. When they stopped to rest for a snack, Frisco took out his pistol and began shooting at some sheep in the distance. "I love to see them scatter," he said. But one or two of the other men came up to him and rebuked him for firing his weapon. They were afraid a patrol might hear it.

When they stopped that evening, Andy and Wally sat together on a large rock discussing how wonderful it would be to reach Spain. "We'll be able to sweat out the rest of the war in a neutral country," said Wally, giving Andy a friendly punch in the ribs.

About that time Frisco came over to them. "The terrain is too difficult to travel safely in the dark," he explained. "Let's stay here for the night, get a good night's rest, and continue on to Spain the next day."

The group spread out among the rocks and settled in for the night, though no one got much sleep. Andy and Wally both wanted to be on their way.

The next morning Frisco awakened everyone and said this would be the day they would push on into Spain. As they began walking, the group spread out. Frisco stayed close to his American companions and about noon announced that the fence line marking the border between Spain and France was just over the next hill.

"You're on your own now. Just walk about two hours, and you will come to a small village, and there you will be taken care of and everything will be all right," Frisco told them.

Andy and Wally thanked him earnestly, assuring this brave man they would do everything in their power to rectify whatever mistakes had been made regarding his passport and return to the United States. He thanked them in return and said he was returning to the captain's house because he had many more American evaders coming through in a few days.

No sooner had he spoken these words than a burst of high-powered gunfire rang out. A large German patrol had spotted them from a distance and was advancing rapidly in their direction.[2]

CHAPTER 26

THE THEATER AND THE STRESS OF POW CAMP: IRV BAUM AND TED BADDER

ife in Stalag Luft III dragged on, each day apparently passing uneventfully yet with a sense that disaster was never far away. Irv Baum later would say that the two things that no POW in Germany ever got accustomed to was realizing his life was at the mercy of someone else and that the Germans seemed to be running out of food to feed their burgeoning prisoner population.

Ted and Irv continued to see each other three or four times a week, even though they were not in the same barracks, usually during their outdoor exercise time. Their shared experiences made the sight of each other somehow comforting, even though both made other friends while in captivity. They often talked about what might have happened to the other guys.

Occasionally they saw Lieutenant Dale Beery, who had been the substitute co-pilot on their mission. But he lived in a barracks on the other side of the compound, and when they caught a glimpse of him, Beery seemed reluctant to speak with them. "What do you think? Think he just doesn't want to get to know us?" Irv asked Ted one day.

"Well, he probably just doesn't feel any connection to our group since he was substituting for our own co-pilot—and Willy, by the way, is overjoyed he wasn't with us that day," said Ted chuckling. "Hey, are you going to the presentation tonight?"

"I guess so. I think the guys are doing some holiday thing since it's that time of the year. But you can bet they won't be doing anything about Hanukkah," said Irv, giving Ted a nudge. Irv often thought about the young German soldier who had signed him into the camp as Protestant.

The presentation that evening was to be given in a room that several men, working for months, had turned into a theater. And somehow, with creativity and imaginative use of materials, they had made it look like a real theater. The prisoners entered the theater through an area that resembled a lobby, in which notices for the camp were posted. The work-men had managed to give the auditorium a pitched floor, as in a real theater, affording good viewing from anywhere in the room. The theater had been constructed with wood packing crates that German guards allowed the prisoners to have. Clothing for costumes and props were scrounged from whatever sources could be found.

It soon became evident that many of the POWs had amateur, or in many cases professional, experience as singers, actors, or musicians. When word spread through the barracks that a theater was being con-structed, these men offered their talents, including one especially nice looking fellow who never minded playing the female roles.

Every couple of months or so, the troops would produce a show—a musical or a series of skits or a comedy routine. Everyone agreed that the productions, under the circumstances, were remarkable. In fact the com-mandant of the camp, Colonel Friedrich Wilhelm von Lindeiner, would often attend, occasionally even bringing his wife.[1]

Such diversions helped the POWs pass the time and keep their spirits up. But not every man could hold it together, as Ted Badder and his barracks-mates found out one morning. The large shower stall at one end of the barracks was sectioned off with a partial wall and curtain. Coming in from their time outdoors, the men noticed the shower had been running a long time. Something seemed wrong. One prisoner walked to the curtain and called out. There was no answer. He waited a moment and called out again. When there was no response a second time, he pulled back the curtain to discover that one of the younger POWs, dressed in the uniform he had arrived in, had hanged himself.

No one in the barracks had much information about him or what had driven him to suicide. One or two said he had seemed somewhat down recently and had talked frequently of how he hated being locked up. But no one had suspected this. The stress of living as a POW often surfaced in unexpected ways.

CHAPTER 27

ONE MORE DAY: GEORGE STARKS

t was during this haul that depression became a serious matter. There had been too many close shaves in too short [a] time: the 20mm hitting the plane, free-falling five miles, the P-47 that had to leave me behind, the discouraging opinions from everyone who helped, the roadblocks, Germans always at hand, not knowing whom to trust, caskets, policemen pointing pistols, roadblocks—but never, never the Underground.

It was very bad. I was cold and hungry and exhausted and scared. Each day I had to make myself go one more day—just like an alcoholic. I'd tell myself that maybe I'd turn myself in tomorrow—but then I'd make myself go one more day.

And each day was the same. My health was dwindling. I had had dark hair when I parachuted into France. I could hardly believe it, but it had begun to grey. Things were really bad. I got what food I could where I could, hid out where I could, but slept very little. I was at the end of my rope.[1]

As George neared Besançon at the edge of the Jura Mountains between France and Switzerland, he tried to stay away from the larger towns. His plan was to circle around Besançon, giving it as wide a berth as possible, then try to rejoin the highway to the southeast. So leaving the main road again, he struck out across the countryside on small lanes.

Many of the inclines were now thirty degrees or more, and snow-drifts often came up to his knees. At these higher altitudes, the temperatures were noticeably colder, and with snow still covering most areas, George's shoes soon became soaked through.

He tried to eat some of the snow at one point just to get a little moisture into his system, and once he found a few berries on a bush. He hoped they were not poisonous, but he was so hungry he ate a handful anyway. His progress was agonizingly slow, and he wasn't sure now exactly where he was.

As he rounded a bend, he spotted a mountain hamlet with a little café. Peering in the window, he didn't see anyone. He was so hungry he decided to take a chance. He went inside, and the proprietor emerged from behind a curtain. George knew he looked like a lost beggar. "I guess I am," he thought to himself.

"Je suis américain," George said. The café owner looked at him and then reached into a cupboard and brought out a small loaf of bread. He handed it to George, who thanked him and left. He knew he had to keep going, but at least he had a little something to eat now.

He continued to push himself, thinking of his one-more-day promise to himself. Take one step, then the next. That night he slept out in the open again.

The next day he got moving before dawn and came across a larger country road down in a narrow valley. Having gone nearly three weeks without adequate food or rest, he decided to follow the road to the next village, Doubs, just north of Pontarlier, another large city he had been told to watch out for because it was filled with Germans.

On the outskirts of Doubs, he spotted a small café, but through the window he could see several German officers inside. They had probably come over from Pontarlier for breakfast. George hastily continued down the village's tight sidewalk, past several small houses and a scattering of shops. At the south end of town, he spied another café and peered inside. Three nuns were sitting with an older man drinking coffee. "Maybe they will help me," he thought to himself. In survival training back in England, they had been told that they could usually count on priests and nuns to help them.

He pushed through the small door and said, "Je suis pilote américain. Parachute en France. Partais à Suisse." It was his usual greeting. With panic on their faces, they motioned frantically for him to leave the café immediately. "Go, go, go away!" they said nearly in unison.

Shocked and confused, George turned and staggered back out onto the sidewalk. He had been certain he had found someone to help him. But he turned and rushed down the sidewalk toward the edge of town, where snowdrifts were deep along the roadside and heavy woods lined both sides ahead of him. Then he stopped, looking at the bleak landscape that lay before him. "Now what?" he asked himself. He stood there for many minutes. "I've had it. This is just too much." He was cold and wet, hungry and exhausted. He felt completely unprepared to face the ordeals that were before him.

"Germans," he thought, "always Germans and never the Underground or Resistance or someone who can actually do something. And now even those nuns turned me away. God, please help me." George had always attended church with his family, and he had always cared deeply for others. But now he prayed with an urgency he had never known before. "I'm alone, deep, deep into occupied France and I need help to escape, God. I can't do this by myself."

It was the lowest point the twenty-year-old had ever known. He was standing ankle-deep in snow and silence lay all around him. Enough, he thought. With that, he turned around and retraced his steps back into Doubs.

CHAPTER 28

STEAMING CLOTHES
ON A STOVE:
GEORGE STARKS CONT'D

George re-entered Doubs and quickly walked past the café where he had been chased away by the nuns. He wasn't sure what he was going to do, but something prompted him to return to the first café to see if there was a back entrance.

As he approached, he didn't see any Germans. He noticed an alleyway that ran alongside the building, and rounding the corner he spotted a door with a large garbage container beside it. He guessed it was the kitchen entrance. There was no window in the door, so he pushed it open slowly. Peering inside, he saw a woman cooking at a large wood-burning stove. She turned toward George and wiped her hands on her apron. With impatience in her voice, she asked him a question in rapid French.

George just stood there, exhausted. A look of recognition came over the woman's face, quickly turning to disbelief. But instead of turning him away, she said quietly, "Rapidement, rapidement," motioning to him to come inside and not to speak. She directed him to remove his soaked clothes, and without any hesitation, he stripped down to his long-handled underwear. For some reason, he decided to leave his beret on. She then pointed to a chair at a small table, arranged the sodden wad of clothes around the stove to dry, and returned to stirring her pot.

George looked around the kitchen. It was full of pots and pans with a few sacks of potatoes and other vegetables. After the woman had stirred the cooking pot several times, she took a piece of black bread from a cupboard and handed it to George. By this time, steam was rising from the clothes drying on the stove.

Neither George nor the woman, who was obviously the owner of the café as well as its cook, spoke. Suddenly the door from the dining room swung open, and a high-ranking German officer walked in. Red stripes ran down the side of his trousers, which were tucked into shiny knee-high boots.

The officer asked the woman something about his food as George sat there in nothing but his underwear, looking down at his bare feet and trying not to appear nervous. She answered, and the officer turned to leave but then stopped at the door and stared for several seconds at George, whose heart was pounding. Then he went back out to the dining area to finish his meal.

For a moment, George thought he was going to be sick. As soon as he could breathe normally again, he looked up at the woman. She gave him the "no talking" sign, and he continued to munch on his bread. She turned back to the stove, pulled down an iron skillet, and broke two fresh eggs into it. In a few minutes, George was eating the best breakfast he had tasted in his life.

The woman remained silent, and George could only guess what was going through her mind. Then the sound of boots and chairs moving came from the dining room, followed by silence. The woman cracked the door open and peeked out. "D'accord, les Boche alléz" she said to George. He understood just enough French to know she meant the Germans had left the café, and they were now safe to talk to one another.

As she returned to her cooking, George recited his well-worn phrase, "Je suis pilote américain. Parachute en France. Partais à Suisse."

Long minutes passed in silence as she continued her chores. He couldn't believe what a close call he had just had. Once again his youthful looks had probably saved him. George hung his head. "There's nothing like sitting in dirty underwear, in the kitchen of a stranger, in a place with the enemy all around," he thought to himself. "I'm really no better off than I was. A little food and maybe a little rest. But too far to go and too many Germans. And still no French Underground." He found himself praying once more: "God, please help me find just one person who can really help me."

Suddenly the back door opened and three Frenchmen walked in. They began talking rapidly with the woman. George was not certain how they knew to come—maybe they were coming to see this woman anyway. Nevertheless, he gathered they were discussing what to do with him and how to help him. He caught enough to know they thought it useless to try to get to Switzerland. "Impossible!" one of the men kept saying.

The men left, and George had never felt so alone and dejected. He had no idea what he was going to do. He knew he couldn't get through Pontarlier, which lay between him and Switzerland, without help. It was still thirty kilometers away and filled with Germans. But he didn't have the strength to bypass it by going through the mountains.

There was a rap on the back door. One of the Frenchmen had returned alone. He and the woman held a fast conversation that George was unable to follow. Next she turned to George and motioned to him to get dressed. He was to follow on a bicycle about a hundred meters behind the Frenchman. If stopped, George was to give no sign of recognition. The woman then showed George a small bicycle in an alcove next to the kitchen door. He did as he was told. His clothes were still damp and foul-smelling, but at least he had some food in his belly.

He followed the man into the center of Doubs, through an iron gate into a walled garden surrounding a two-story house. After George cycled inside, the man hurriedly shut the gate behind them.

"Quick! Quick! Upstairs!" the man said in urgent but quiet tones. George climbed the outside staircase as rapidly as he could. The Frenchman, who sported an impressive mustache, then closed and locked the door behind them. His name was Henri Chambelland, and to George's disbelief, he turned out to be the chief of police of Doubs.

Then a door on one side of the room opened, and one of the prettiest girls George had ever laid eyes on came in. The police chief introduced his eighteen-year-old daughter, Giselle, to the gaping American pilot, who regretted he only knew three sentences in French.

CHAPTER 29

THE CHIEF OF POLICE AND GISELLE: GEORGE STARKS CONT'D

Henri Chambelland, though head of the police department, wore civilian clothes, usually a suit with a tie and a natty vest. He told George he could stay at his house while he tried to find some way to help him. It was music to George's ears. He needed to rest and he needed food. The head of the gendarmes in Doubs then told his daughter to lead their guest to a small bedroom at the rear of their apartment.

When Giselle showed George into the bedroom, he felt like he was in heaven. There was an iron bed covered with a handmade quilt and a chest with a hurricane lamp. The warm sunshine streamed in through a window with lace café curtains.

Giselle spoke softly in French, smiling all the time and giving the young pilot friendly glances as she showed him around. Then she pointed to his dirty clothes and with gestures explained what she wanted him to do—undress. George smiled back, and she stepped out of the room, waiting behind the door. He quickly shimmied out of everything this time, including his long-handled underwear and beret. Then he pulled back the covers on the iron bed and dove beneath the quilt. "Okay," he called to Giselle, and the pretty young girl, still smiling and glancing sideways at him, came in and gathered up his pile of filthy clothes. George grinned at her as she left the room with his clothes, then he rolled over and immediately fell sound asleep.

When he awakened, it was approaching dusk outside. "Good grief," he thought, "I must have slept all day." He had been tired to the bone. Somehow, however, he felt safe with the chief of police.

Soon there was a quiet knock on the door. M. Chambelland opened it slightly and looked in. He was holding a pair of pants and a clean but worn shirt. "For you," he said and handed the clothes to George.

George thanked him, and the Frenchman explained in spotty English that his own clothes would be ready the following morning. Then he told George to get dressed and come with him. They had something for him to eat. The evader followed his new "helper" into a parlor where a round dining table was set for dinner. Giselle brought in a bowl filled with soup, and George thought he had never smelled anything so good. The three of them sat down, and M. Chambelland bowed his head to say a blessing. Then Giselle served the soup, which was really more like a meat stew. There was also fresh bread with homemade preserves and coffee. To the starving American, it was a feast.

As they ate, George explained as well as he could what had happened to him, where he had been, and how he was trying desperately to reach Switzerland. Like so many others, Chambelland thought trying to cross the Swiss border was not a good idea. But George kept saying that he had already come so far. He just couldn't turn back now.

After they finished their meal, the chief of police explained that the following morning he was going to try to make arrangements for George. He would be gone most of the day, and he wanted George to stay in the house, keeping quiet and away from the windows.

After the dishes had been cleared from the table, George suddenly felt weak, as if he were going to be overcome with sleep right there at the table. He told his host and his pretty daughter that he was simply worn out. They waved him back to his bedroom. George undressed and climbed back into the soft bed. He remembered nothing else until clear sunshine was streaming through the window once again the following morning.

As he lay in the bed, the first one he had slept on in many days, it occurred to him that meeting M. Chambelland was an answer to his desperate prayers, though he remained uncertain what, if anything, this man could do for him. George didn't know exactly where he was, but he knew he was close to the border. From here to Switzerland, he realized, would be the hardest part of his journey because the Germans would certainly be guarding this area with vigilance.

About that time there came a light tap at his door. "Entre," said George.

The door quietly opened, and Giselle stood there grinning at him again. The dark-haired beauty held a stack of his clothes, clean and perfectly folded. "Voici vos vêtements," she said, and laid them on top of the dresser. Looking at him once more, she turned and left the bedroom. George was certain this must be what heaven was like. He got up and dressed.

He thought about the people who had given him these clothes, and how somebody else he didn't really know was washing them and helping to keep him clean. "So many people have helped me—it's really amazing. Someday I hope I can do something for them," he thought to himself.

He spent the day resting and talking to Giselle. Though language was a barrier, it did not stop communication completely. She was quick to catch on to his pointing and few French words. And though their conversation was limited, the young man and woman relished each other's company.

When M. Chambelland returned that night, he told George that the next morning he would take him to meet someone—in Pontarlier. George knew the city was crawling with Germans, and he had been told to avoid it. But M. Chambelland insisted, explaining how they would ride their bicycles into the city, George trailing behind him at a distance of at least a hundred meters.

George had no choice but to trust this man. The next morning when he awoke, he experienced that fatigue that was nearly overpowering when he had to leave a place that had offered a sense of security. He could easily have stayed right there in the cozy bedroom with its iron bed, its window full of sunshine, and a pretty young girl to wash his clothes and speak softly to him in French.

The two men struck out on their bicycles. George waved to Giselle and wondered if he would ever see her again.

It was only a three-kilometer ride to the city. From the moment they entered its outskirts, it was evident that Pontarlier was filled with Germans, but George kept pedaling. He had no choice. Several times he was on the verge of losing M. Chambelland, but he somehow stuck with him through the crowded streets.

Pontarlier was an old city with a walled marketplace. Chambelland turned into a gateway in the wall, stopped, parked his bicycle, crossed the cobblestone street, and entered a small bakery on the other side. George felt his adrenaline surging again. He waited a moment, then he too parked his bicycle, crossed the narrow street, and entered the bakery, the bell above the door announcing his entrance.

He found himself inside a small room, perhaps ten feet by twelve feet, a wonderful yeast aroma filling the air, where a woman behind a glass case was wrapping some baked goods for her customer—a German officer. George stopped in his tracks. His guide was nowhere to be seen. The German took his purchase and turned to leave. He looked straight at George, who pretended to be examining some rolls stacked inside the case, then walked out the door, its bell ringing once again.

As soon as the officer left, the woman motioned for George to follow her through a curtained doorway into the kitchen. There sat Chambelland with a man in a white coat, presumably the baker, and a tall, slim Frenchman who seemed to command the room with his very presence though he said nothing. The three men began a fast conversation, while the woman stood next to the curtain looking out into the shop.

Even though the three men were not looking at him, George could tell that he was the topic of their conversation. He grasped a few words here and there, and then it dawned on him: the tall, slim man was a member of the Free French. Noticing the deference that the other two men showed to him, George presumed he was an important person. Someone with connections, with an organized group within resistance circles—what he had prayed and hoped for throughout the weeks of fear and discouragement—was sitting right in front of his eyes.

It was Maurice Baverel, whom George would one day call the bravest man he ever knew.

CHAPTER 30

A TRAIN FULL OF GERMANS: GEORGE STARKS CONT'D

"**D**o you ski?" he asked, with a heavy French accent. The slim but muscular man was only six years George's senior but appeared much older—seasoned like a street dog that knows his way around compared with a house pet, George thought. Maurice Baverel was sizing up the new "project" standing before him.

"Well…no. No, I don't snow ski. I'm from Florida—I can water ski though," said George, hoping that would count for something.

Maurice took a long drag from his cigarette and continued eyeing the younger man. "Well, how do you expect to get to Switzerland if you don't ski?" he asked.

George felt as if the floor was moving beneath him, shifting out of place. His heart sank. "Well…I dunno," replied George, crestfallen. Was this going to be a dead end too?

Maurice again looked him up and down then leaned back in his chair. Suddenly he broke into a wide grin. "Not to worry," he said. "We find a way." With that, Maurice stood up and told George, "Come." Saying good-bye to Chambelland and the baker, he made his way to the front door, waving at George to follow.

Maurice and George left the bakery and emerged onto the sidewalk, now filled with German soldiers coming and going in all directions. When they reached a spot without any other pedestrians close by, George leaned in close to Maurice. "Don't you want me to follow behind?" George spoke in pidgin French, but Maurice seemed to understand. He looked at George.

"What, did the other helpers make you do so? They were afraid. No, no. You walk beside me. I talk; you pretend to listen. Nod your head, and when I laugh, you laugh." Maurice seemed perfectly comfortable to have his ward walking right next to him through the crowd, so the two of them worked their way through the streets. Maurice continued to talk and laugh; George continued to nod and laugh along.

George Starks

We must have looked like a pair. Me in my baggy pants, dirty, buttoned-up trench coat. Maurice, natty really, with long black hair in a pompadour, neat clothes, clean and pressed. He was not imposing but certainly well built.

Anyway, we laughed and nodded our way toward the center of the city to the train station. Maurice said we would simply get on a train and go to the small village of Les Hôpitaux-Neufs near the border. There he said his uncle had a home where we could headquarter and would figure out things from there.

The Pontarlier train station was swarming with more Germans than I had ever seen before: officers, troops with packs and rifles, and very few civilians.

We pushed through the crowd of them, and Maurice worked our way to the station café. He sat the two of us at a crowded table right in the middle of an ocean of German officers eating lunch. I mean, they were sitting at each elbow.

Maurice ordered coffee for me, but he had a local version of white lightning, made from potatoes, I think. And we sat there with him telling stories, me pretending to understand, laughing when he laughed. His were words blended into the noise and bustle of the station.

Then he got up and walked away to get tickets. He just walked away leaving me sitting alone in that mass of soldiers. He knew full well that a bad move on my part would finish us both.

The man had nerve, that's for sure. He came back with the tickets, grabbed me in tow, and we went out to the loading platform.

The train we boarded was a short five-car affair pulled by a small wood-burning locomotive. We had seats on the second or third car, I forget which, but we were the only civilians there.

Anyway, we went chugging out of the station and started climbing the twisting, narrow gauge rails up through the mountains. It wasn't a bad ride, really—the small cars rocking and clattering along, the little engine tooting its steam whistle. And beyond our steamed glass windows, the snow-filled mountains. We could have been like tourists chatting away and sightseeing if there hadn't been so many Germans.

We pulled into the small station at the village of Les Hôpitaux-Neufs and stood up to join the aisle full of detraining Germans. We were inching our way forward with the crowd, when we noticed that each carload was not debarking by its own door. They were making the entire trainload disembark through the front coach and we saw guards there, carefully checking papers. There was no way I could bluff my way past that kind of check; we were the only civilians in sight.

Maurice took the situation in at a glance. He turned around as if he had left a package on his seat, and pulled me after him. The two *of us pushed against that flow of Germans, through one car past into the next car, and then to the last car on the train.*

That coach was now empty. And at its far end was a door exiting away from the station side of the train. Maurice went to it, opened that thing up, and we just jumped down and walked through the snow up the hill and away from the station.

I just couldn't believe my eyes! Maurice just opened the door, and we simply walked away. The man had more guts than anyone I'd ever seen.[1]

CHAPTER 31

MAURICE BAVEREL, A SPY FOR ALL SEASONS: GEORGE STARKS CONT'D

George followed Maurice up a gentle rolling hill, then down into the next village. They stopped at a charming house, its yard lined with shrubs, at the end of a lane off the main street. There was a white picket fence across the front and steps leading to a porch on the second story. Underneath was a garage at street level. The house overlooked the train station, which was teeming with Germans. The village, covered with what was left of the winter's snow, was filled with trucks and soldiers riding motorcycles.

Maurice knocked on the front door, and he and George were admitted to a homey living room by Maurice's uncle Henri Boillot and his wife, Nanny. They instantly took a liking to the personable young American, and George found their hospitality warm and friendly. Nanny made coffee and produced a plate of thin lemon cookies. They settled into overstuffed chairs, and George, for the first time in many days, actually felt somewhat safe.

The Boillots, who spoke better English than Maurice did, told George about themselves. Henri, a schoolmaster, had lived in that area of France all his life. Maurice was the son of his sister, and he had watched him grow up. Both Henri and Nanny seemed delighted to have George in their home. They conversed for quite a while in French with Maurice about George's situation. George heard "Suisse" mentioned several times and knew they were probably discussing the difficulties of helping him across the border. He also heard Maurice saying something about his inability to ski, and George decided skiing must be the primary way to cross over.

Early the next morning, Maurice left to work on getting George into Switzerland without skis. George spent the day visiting with the Boillots and sometimes with their son, a doctor in a neighboring village. Everyone in the family, he found, was knowledgeable and well traveled. He also learned a great deal about Maurice Baverel, who was part of the French Resistance but also fed information to the British and American intelligence services through the British consul in Switzerland.

A man of astonishing courage, Maurice had once led four comrades in an intense firefight against forty Germans. After two of his men had run away and another one had been killed, Maurice was down to one round, which he was saving for himself. At the last moment, forty more Resistance fighters showed up, and the Frenchmen captured the twenty-eight Germans who were still alive.

Several days before the Allied invasion of Normandy, Maurice had ridden the trains along the coastline non-stop for ten days, memorizing German troop numbers, guns placements, and the general movement of arms and materiel, information he then delivered to Allied intelligence officers in Switzerland.

He had been captured twice by the Germans—once because a comrade had broken under torture and revealed where Maurice was staying. When the betrayer, encountering Maurice in prison, begged for forgiveness, Maurice told him not to worry about it. "At least they will no longer mistreat you," he said. He and his cellmates soon escaped by sharpening their metal spoons into chisels and loosening the bars of the windows. Maurice then "rode the rods" back to his hometown, a perilous maneuver that involved balancing on the truss rods underneath a boxcar for hours at a time.

Having grown up in the area around his uncle's house, familiar with every stream and boulder, Maurice was an expert at crossing the border. Besides taking information across to the Allies, he often smuggled people, including a dozen U.S. servicemen. He guided an entire Dutch family on skis, evading the German patrols under cover of a nighttime blizzard. It took twelve hours to cover the one kilometer between the town of Jougne and the Swiss border, but they made it safely across without incident.

Such an escape would be impossible for George, since the Florida boy didn't ski—at least not on snow. Maurice presented the problem to the military attaché at the American embassy in Bern, Switzerland, asking if they could send some people to get him out. But such a rescue, in the attaché's view, would be too dangerous for everyone involved. Perhaps, he suggested, a small plane could land near the Boillot residence if a big enough field could be found. When Maurice returned to his uncle's house several days later, he and George began looking for a suitable field, but every open space was too short, too rocky, or too steep. It seemed to George that he was right back where he had started.[1]

George Starks

An airplane seemed the only apparent way out, and we just couldn't find a place for one to land. Switzerland was only eight kilometers away but there might just as well have been an ocean between me and there.

And I knew my time at the schoolmaster's house was running out. I had been with them nearly two weeks. Again, just too many Germans. I could easily see the troops boarding and de-boarding at the train station from my bedroom window.

And with the border so near, the area was heavily patrolled. I could be spotted at any time, and while I was certainly comfortable, my hosts and I were still in grave danger.

Anyway, Maurice and I couldn't find a landing area. Then Maurice remembered a large lake nearby. It was wide enough for a floatplane and would now be free of ice. He decided to propose the idea to the military attaché the next time he went across to Switzerland.

The American military in Lausanne nixed the idea of trying to fly a floatplane in—it was just too dangerous to put a plane down on the water at night with mountains all around. When Maurice came back he told me they had rejected the idea.

So escape by plane was out. Only the road was left, and it was heavily patrolled and there were too many roadblocks. I was really nervous about it all, but I had confidence in Maurice—it was impossible not to have confidence in Maurice.

Little did I know, however, that the worst moments of the entire six weeks of my attempt to escape into Switzerland were still to come.[2]

CHAPTER 32

DR. CHARLIN AND THE FIVE-HORSEPOWER PEUGEOT: GEORGE STARKS CONT'D

Maurice knew he had to find another plan. Henri told him about a doctor, Paul Charlin, three kilometers to the south, just past the border town of Jougne, who he suspected was working with the Underground. George knew that Resistance fighters were highly secretive—they had to be. Unless you had actually worked with someone on an operation, there was no way to know for sure. But Maurice intended to find out.[1]

Under the pretense that his wife was ill, Henri asked Dr. Charlin to come to his house. The next morning, the doctor puttered over in his old five-horsepower Peugeot. Since he was the only doctor in the region, Charlin was one of the few civilians the Germans allowed to have a car and a measure of gasoline with which to make his calls.

As soon as Dr. Charlin stepped inside, Maurice said, "I am with the Resistance. Are you?"

"The name of the dog," the doctor answered—the code for "Yes, I am." Maurice shook his hand, the two men looked at each other for a moment, and Maurice told him about the American pilot who couldn't ski whom he was trying to get across the border into Switzerland. Then Maurice summoned George from upstairs, where he had waited until Maurice knew whether the doctor could be trusted. The doctor said simply, "I will hide him in the back of my car and take him with me to a house I know about right near the border. I'll wait until I think the danger is the least."

The plan was just that simple—and just that dangerous.

After Dr. Charlin had gone, Maurice also left, saying he would return the following day.

That night, George found talking to Henri and Nanny as pleasant as usual, but he was melancholy—and nervous. He had been with them nearly twelve days now, and he knew it was time to leave. Each time he experienced the generosity of his French helpers, he hated to leave his refuge—now perhaps more than before. The Boillots were remarkable for their kindness and sunny dispositions. Henri, George learned, was not only a schoolmaster but also an artist, who depicted the French countryside in beautiful watercolors. But George knew what a great personal risk they were taking to help him. "God, I hope nothing happens to them because of what they are doing," he thought. "And I hope we are able to get to the house of Dr. Charlin's contact without getting caught." Wondering if he would ever see the Boillots again, George felt anxious all day long.

The next morning, Dr. Charlin pulled into the garage. He and Maurice, who had returned the night before, hustled George out of the house and onto the floorboard behind the seats. The doctor threw a blanket over him and piled his medical bag and a few instruments on top.

"We have four roadblocks we must get through," he told George. "You must stay perfectly still all the way." With his secret cargo concealed on the floorboard, he climbed into the driver's seat, backed out of the Boillot garage, and chugged off.

George Starks

As we drew near the first roadblock, the doctor whispered back to me that I wasn't to move a single muscle, not even to breathe. I have never been more scared in my life.

I could hear Dr. Charlin slowing the car and rolling down the window. The guard stepped up to the window and asked to see his papers. I could hear everything that was going on from under the blanket and I expected the guard to yank it off any second.

Then the doctor was cleared. He put the car into gear, and we drove on.

A second roadblock—the same procedure. As soon as he stopped the car, I tried not to breathe at all.

We drove a little further down the bumpy road as fast as his five-horsepower Peugeot could manage. Outrunning anything if we were caught would have been impossible.

I could feel the car slowing down once more—a third roadblock. Each time, the guard asked for the doctor's papers, and the doctor explained he was going to his house. Perhaps they were accustomed to his coming and going to see patients—I don't know, but we had now successfully cleared our third roadblock—only one more to go.

"Please let this work," I kept praying.

I could feel the car slowing down once more. I could hear the window rolling down, but this time it seemed the guard kept standing beside the car. I couldn't determine what was happening because I couldn't hear anything. I wondered if he was looking into the back at the blanket and medical supplies.

The seconds seemed to be dragging by. Dr. Charlin said something rather gruffly and the guard seemed to relent]… because the next thing I knew, that old five-horsepower car was cranking up again and we were on our way.

Miraculously we had made it through four roadblocks without being detected. Now if we could just make it to the house that Dr. Charlin was taking me to.

Shortly I could feel the car driving over gravel. The doctor stopped and without saying a word to me, got out of the car, leaving me under the blanket.

He returned about two minutes later and hastily removed his medical bag and supplies, then the coverlet, and told me to go as quickly as possible into the house.

Waiting for us inside was none other than Maurice himself. He had skied overland and without having to go through roadblocks had beaten us there. Maurice said we could hide here until it was safe to cross over. The house was owned by a couple who had a twelve-year-old son. All three seemed accustomed to this arrangement—uneasy but not unfamiliar with what was going on.

Now I was temporarily safe again. But it could not go on long—too many patrols passing by. I knew every minute I was there, I posed an incredible threat to the doctor and this family.

I could look out the window and down the slope and see Switzerland. The border at this point was not fenced or fortified, but it was heavily patrolled by teams of German guards with their dogs.

That made Switzerland still a long way ahead, and we had to cross at exactly the right moment—when a patrol was not in sight. The odds seemed completely against us.[2]

PART IV

THE FINAL PUSH OUT

CHAPTER 33

WORSENING CONDITIONS: IRV BAUM AND TED BADDER

B y January 1945, nearly a year after Irv Baum and Ted Badder had been captured, the POWs at Stalag Luft III were seeing evidence that the war was drawing to a close. For several weeks, rumors of the end had been running through the camp, but there were physical signs as well—food was beginning to get very scarce, and guards were being transferred out with no replacements for them coming in.

One bitterly cold day shortly after New Year's, the inmates thought they could hear cannon in the distance. "Do you suppose that's the Russians coming?" Ted asked Irv one morning as they huddled together outside their barracks, shaking their arms and rubbing their hands together. The snow had lightened some, but the ground was already covered with several inches. They were in the middle of Germany's coldest winter of the twentieth century.

"Don't know. What do you think the Krauts are going to do with us?" replied Irv.

"Yeah—that's the question," said Ted. The buddies wished each other well and headed back inside their barracks.

On January 19, the guards awakened all the POWs in the middle of the night and ordered them to get dressed immediately and gather up their belongings. The camp was being evacuated; they would depart in an hour. The same thing was happening in all the other POW camps in northeastern Germany. The men were about to embark on a nightmarish forced march in sub-zero temperatures with no winter clothing or boots.

Irv emerged from his barracks at about one o'clock in the morning as the servicemen were forming up six or so abreast. Together with the guards, they set out down a deserted road through a forest thick with tall trees and underbrush.

Irv didn't see Ted anywhere. It appeared that the prisoners—there were now several thousand at Stalag Luft III—were leaving the camp in groups of roughly two hundred at a time, and he wondered where they were headed. Irv's group walked for four or five hours and then was allowed to rest. He took out a few crackers and a little cheese from his knapsack, thankful to have anything at all to eat. As morning dawned fully, the guards signaled for them to start again.

The march through heavily wooded areas with steep inclines took nearly three days and ended at Spremberg, a small town fifty-five miles away. Here the POWs were boarded onto a train. It felt so good to be out of the weather and to be able to sit down. Irv learned from another POW who had overheard the guards talking among themselves that they were headed to another prisoner of war camp much farther south. Their destination was Stalag VII-A, just north of Moosburg in southern Bavaria, some 340 miles away.

The train rumbled on, filled with POWs and guards. By this time, many of the captives were suffering from hunger and exposure. For several weeks before this move, their meals had been noticeably paltry, often nothing more than a bowl of thin soup. Irv looked around the compartment he was riding in. Every inch was packed. Men sat crushed together on the floor, down the aisles, in the corners. When he was able to catch a glimpse out the windows, it appeared the train was pulling several cars, each overflowing with POWs. Again, he thought about his crewmate Ted Badder and wondered where he was.

When the train finally came to a stop, the POWs walked to their new prison, where they encountered unimaginable conditions. The camp, built to house around five thousand prisoners, now overflowed with more than a hundred thousand men and some women from all over the globe, some of them not even military but journalists or radio operators. The American POWs here numbered around forty-five thousand.

When Irv entered one of the barracks, men stood nearly shoulder-to-shoulder in the rooms. Everyone was talking about what this might mean, where the Allies were, and when they might be liberated. But as always, all optimism was mixed with caution. There was simply no way to guess what might happen in the weeks ahead.

As the spring of 1945 unfolded and the prisoners' worst fears about their rations were realized, they knew the end of the war must be near. But how the Germans might react to their impending defeat was anybody's guess. During the first couple weeks in April, the unmistakable sounds of battle could be heard. Heavy artillery and gunfire seemed to come from all directions.

Since Allied forces had no idea of the size of the POW camp, they sent only a dozen or so soldiers to liberate it. They were shocked to be met by nearly three hundred armed guards, who allowed the American troops to disarm them and pile their weapons in a central heap until more Allies arrived. As the POWs began leaving the camp, the incoming American soldiers were inundated with cheering, whistling, and shouts of joy. The freed captives swarmed over the tanks until they looked like anthills.

Amazingly enough, Irv and Ted found each other, grabbing each other's hands and arms, and Irv yelled, "Man, this is it, Ted, it's really it!"

"Buddy, it is so good to see you again too," said Ted.

As they stood together, a wave of excitement rippled through the crowd. The men parted for a jeep bearing a red tag with four stars. "It's General Patton," somebody yelled. Irv and Ted recognized him from pictures and newsreels. He was wearing a leather bomber jacket and the most highly polished knee boots Irv had ever seen. The general stopped his jeep, and the crowd of POWs immediately closed in around it.

"Good to see you, boys!" he yelled. The cheering was deafening and lasted for what seemed an eternity. Patton continued to call out to the crowds of POWs representing every nation that had taken part in the fight. Finally he slapped his helmet and directed his driver to continue on. The jubilation didn't stop as the jeep slowly wound its way up the road headed due north. "We're on our way to Berlin!" he could be heard yelling over the celebrating men.

As the two crewmen, along with hundreds of other liberated POWs, began to walk down the road in the opposite direction toward the advancing army, a Red Cross truck rolled up to them and stopped.

The driver yelled out, "Hey, any of you willing to come help us? We've got a mess on our hands over at another camp that was just liberated yesterday. Not enough regular soldiers to help us. We sure could use you. We've got bodies to sort through. They are mainly Jewish people who died in the camp."

Irv looked at Ted. "You go on ahead. I'll go help and catch up with you later." As Irv climbed into the truck, another POW, an enlisted man who was also Jewish, said he would volunteer too. Neither had any idea what he was about to witness.

Driving along, the Red Cross worker explained they were headed to a concentration camp called Dachau. He said thousands of people, mainly Jews, had been imprisoned there, and the Germans had left the dead bodies piled up.

"But here's what has happened. After the Russians liberated one of these camps farther north, a place called Treblinka, they had brought in heavy equipment to help shovel away the dead bodies. They had already started when they discovered three people in the pile who were still breathing. Can you believe that?" The Red Cross workers were obviously distressed and running on adrenaline. Irv couldn't believe what he was hearing. "So orders came down banning the use of bulldozers because there might be others still alive. We are tasked with going through the bodies by hand." They were speeding along the country road as fast as columns of soldiers, tanks, and other advancing military traffic would allow.

Irv looked over at the enlisted guy who had also volunteered. Their eyes met, and they stared at each other for a moment. Irv looked away, filled with emotion.

When they arrived at the camp, Irv emerged from the truck and couldn't believe what he saw. It was one of the largest facilities he had ever seen. Row after row of barracks filled the muddy fields, a wasteland of trash piles scattered here and there. Wisps of smoke wafted upward into the air, thick with the smell of death and decay.

Immediately Red Cross workers came up to him and the several other volunteers who had come to help. They wrapped ankle-length grey gowns around each of them. Then the volunteers were provided gloves, masks, and paper head coverings. As soon as they were robed, a worker began rubbing DDT down the fronts and backs of the gowns.

Irv glanced around and saw several other soldiers who evidently had also volunteered to shuffle through the mounds of bodies looking for anyone who might still be alive. As he walked toward the areas where they would be working he stopped, dumbfounded by what he saw.

A large group of Red Cross members sat with at least a hundred children, ranging from about five years old to teenagers. There was an eerie silence hanging over the entire group. None of the boys and girls, dirty and dressed in rags, made any noise. Their faces were empty and staring, as if in shock.

The Red Cross workers were trying to feed some of them with eye droppers. Some of the most despondent ones were just being held and rocked. Irv had never seen anything so heartbreaking in his life. He guessed these were children of people who had been interned in the camp, and his guess was later confirmed.

As he walked on, the Red Cross workers pointed him to a pile of bodies that were no more than bones covered with thin layers of skin. Even through his mask he could barely breathe without gagging. Irv began pulling at the bodies, separating them in order to see if any showed signs of life. Most of them, however, were already in some stage of decomposition.

After working about an hour or so, Irv could not go on. The crash of his B-17 nearly fifteen months previously, the frantic capture and injury to his eye, the nights enduring fake executions, and the months and months in a POW camp with meager food rations, never knowing for certain what the outcome might be—the cumulative misery of all these events suddenly came crashing down upon him. The sight of these bodies was overwhelming. He turned and walked toward the nearest Red Cross truck, jerking off his mask, gown, and gloves. "I'm sorry," he said choking back his emotions. "I just can't do this anymore." He turned and began walking down the road toward the Allied lines.

CHAPTER 34

THE BLACK DEATH MARCH: DICK MORSE

A t the beginning of 1945, the war was going badly for the Germans. The Russian army was approaching from the East, and the Americans and British were ready to overrun their country.

In late January, after we had been at Stalag Luft IV for about five months, all of the sickly prisoners in the camp were shipped out—supposedly to be repatriated—and there were rumors that we would be leaving the camp. One day a wagonload of new GI shoes were dumped on the ground, and anyone who wanted a pair could take them, so I hunted through the pile and found some that fit me.

On February 6, 1945, the lights in our barracks came on at about two a.m., and the guards ordered us to hurry and get our things together. We didn't have much. I put a pair of khaki pants over my GI wool pants. They both had button flies, which I knew would not be very convenient, but at least they would help to keep me warm.

Then I rolled up my blanket, tied it with a shoestring, and bent it into the shape of a horseshoe, so I could carry it by placing it around my neck and have my hands free. We were all weak due to malnutrition and not prepared to survive the cold winter weather.

At daybreak we were ready to leave. It was snowing, the wind was blowing, and it was almost zero. There were about six thousand prisoners, and we left in increments of two thousand. We plodded along through about fourteen inches of snow, four or five abreast, heading West away from the Russian army.

We were told that we were going to travel for three days to another camp, but there were many rumors flying around. Among them was [one] that we were going to be used as pawns in negotiations so the Germans could get a better deal; another was that Hitler had ordered that our clothing be taken away and to send us in a march in freezing winter weather. As we traveled the groups got smaller, because some would branch off and take different directions.

There was a horse-drawn wagon that traveled with us, and if anyone became ill, collapsed, or became exhausted, he could get on and ride. But at times, for some unknown reason, we did not have a horse, so prisoners would take turns pulling the wagon.

When POWs became weak and could not keep up with the group, other POWs would help them along, and if they lagged too far behind, often they would be gun-butted by the guards. When the wagon was not available or was full and a POW could not keep up with the group, a German would drop back and take him into the bushes or woods. We would hear a shot—then the guard would return alone.

Food was a hit-or-miss situation. Most days no food was provided, but occasionally we might get a little sawdust bread, which was thrown from a wagon onto the ground. Usually we had to scrounge for our food and at times found frozen carrots, kohlrabies, or onions in the fields or stored in barns.

Joe Wagner, Hugh Wier, a fellow named Watson, and I had a buddy system. We had a can and would put some water in it with the vegetables we had, build a small fire, and make some soup, but there were times when we were not allowed to have a fire.

We had been warned by Dr. Caplan, a doctor who was also a POW, not to drink any water from streams along the way, because we could get dysentery or other diseases. But there were no other sources for water. Most of us simply couldn't continue without some water, so we did drink and almost every day got dysentery.

There was no medication available—we used ashes from our fire for relief. Because of a lack of food sources and the extreme weather conditions, it would be foolish to try to escape, and we had been warned by the guards that we would be shot if we tried. Many nights we went to bed hungry, woke up hungry, and were hungry all day.

We traveled going in one direction and then another, and eventually came to the realization that we really had no destination but were just kept moving along. We marched from the Eastern Front to the Western Front and then doubled back to the Eastern Front and every night had to find a place to sleep.

At times we found a barn and were able to sleep inside, and if there was hay in it, it was more comfortable. Often the farmers would not let us in their barns, because we might contaminate the hay and then the cows wouldn't eat it, and they also did not want the animals to get our body lice and fleas.

If there were no barns around, we slept in the fields or forest and never took our clothes off, and if they got wet they would freeze. Our shoes got wet and muddy, but we didn't take them off because if they froze, we would be unable to get them back on. When the wind was blowing and it was snowing, we put our blanket over our head and shoulders, leaving a hole to see through. It has been said that the winter of 1944–45 was the coldest winter in Europe in the century.

On Valentine's Day, February 14, 1945, about a week after leaving the camp, it was a wet snowy day. At about four p.m. it was getting dark, and we came to a clearing. There were about fifty of us in the group, and we took a rest beside the road.

Captain Caplan, who did everything he possibly could for all of us, stopped to talk to us. He said this was a deplorable situation. There was no food and no place to stay that night, so we would have to sleep out in the snow-covered fields. Joe and I found an old tree trunk, put our blankets over us, and went to sleep. I believe it was the most miserable night I ever spent—bitter cold and wet all over.

At daybreak, we moved on toward Peenemünde and along the way saw some German V-2 rockets behind some fences, ready to be fired. We came to a ferry and crossed the straights.

One windy March day, we came to a barn and I could hear some cows inside. I was so hungry and thirsty I decided to try to milk a cow, but left in a hurry when I was struck on my back by a guard.

Another time, we came out of the woods into a clearing and were walking down the road, when suddenly two British planes flew toward us, then passed and circled back, coming toward us at full power, shooting all the way up the road.

We all ran to the side of the road and flattened ourselves in a ditch, and when we thought we had a chance, we ran for a nearby barn and found a chimney to stand by. When we finally came outside, we found a horse that had been hit and we used it for food. As we straggled along in a group, we apparently had been mistaken for a group of German soldiers and were a target opportunity.

Another time, as we were traveling through a village where there were buildings lining the road but no sidewalks, a horse and wagon came tearing down the road. Apparently the horse was out of control, and the wagon was rocking from side to side. We had no place to go, so we all flattened ourselves against doorways.

One day we came to a POW camp in Fallingbostel and stopped to see if we could get some food and rest for a while. They had no food either and it was very crowded, so we had to move along.

Our guards were mostly old men, some disabled and unable to fight in the regular army, and at times they were hanged. One of them told us he had a son who was being held in a POW camp in Arizona and that he was being treated very well. He appreciated it very much, he said.

One guard, who was nicknamed "Big Stoop," was exceptionally mean. He was a big man with very large hands, which he would use to whuck the POWs on the side of the head in such a way that he would puncture their ear drums.

Diseases such as pneumonia, diphtheria, typhus, trench foot, tuberculosis, and dysentery ran rampant; blisters, abscesses, and frostbite became epidemic. To quote Dr. Caplan, as a medical expert, "The march was nightmarish." Our sanitation approached medieval standards, and the inevitable result was disease, suffering, and death. If someone was so ill that he could not continue on, he often had to be left in a barn in hopes that someone would come along and help him.[1]

After we had traveled for about three months and covered approximately six hundred miles, sleeping in barns with rats running around or outside in all kinds of winter weather, sometimes with snow almost up to our knees, and little nourishment, I was determined I would never give up. I was dirty, tired, hungry, and had dysentery, lice, and fleas, but I really believed I would get home. My shoes, which were new when I started out, were almost worn out. Some days we would travel many miles with little food and rest, but I was fortunate. I had always been able to walk, and I never had to hitch a ride on the wagon.

On May 2, 1945, as we plodded along—I believe near Zarrentin, Germany—two British sergeants in a recon car drove up to us, and our German guards simply threw down their guns. At last the march was over...and I think our guards were just as relieved as we were.[2]

CHAPTER 35

A SMALL MIRACLE:
ANDY BRENDEN AND
WALLY TRINDER

When the Germans opened fire, the group trying to cross through the Pyrenees into Spain frantically scattered, looking for places to hide. Andy and Wally, gasping for breath, kept low to avoid the flying bullets that seemed to be everywhere and inched their way toward the fenced border, so enticingly close.

Andy grabbed Wally. "Do you think if we just hunker down somewhere we could hide long enough, so they wouldn't find us?"

"I don't think that would help," said Wally. They looked around and could see several of the other men trying to stay down.

Then they heard barking, and three large German police dogs charged up the incline straight toward them. One of the dogs lunged at a Frenchman in the group, who pulled a knife and slit its throat. Frisco shot the second dog, which had grabbed him by the leg. The third dog suddenly spooked and ran back in the direction it had come from. The engagements with the dogs allowed the Germans to adjust their range, and their fire became more accurate. Andy began pushing himself across the ground with a stick, trying to make some progress up the hill, when the stick was shot out from his hand. "This is it," he thought. "It's all over." Just then, Wally caught up with him and yelled, "We've got to make a run for it!" They looked at each other.

"You're right. We've come too far to get beat now," said Andy with determination.

They began running in a zigzag pattern, interspersed with rolling on the ground. The German fire was not as accurate as when the two men were trying to run in a straight line. Andy saw the soldiers circling around the side of the hill, trying to cut them off at the border. The low wire fence separating France from Spain was just in front of them. They had been told that once they crossed it, the Germans would stop shooting at them, but now the bullets were whizzing again, and they had to duck behind a large boulder.

"We've got to make a dash for it," said Wally. Just then a bullet hit the rock, shearing off a piece that tore into Andy's kneecap. The pain was searing, but for the moment he was too afraid for his life to stop. "You've been hit!" yelled Wally.

"Yeah but we can't stop now," answered Andy. "They'll either kill us or throw us into a concentration camp. We've got to try. Come on."

They ran as fast as they could toward the fence, Andy barely noticing how badly hurt his leg was. They climbed over the wire and looked back to see the Germans circling around the top of the hill on the French side. In front of them was a steep incline covered with snow, and the Germans continued firing even though the two Americans were now in Spain.

"They must be running low on ammo, 'cause they're being really careful with their shots," Andy yelled to Wally. The two of them looked back up behind them. Two German soldiers were taking aim at them from higher up on the hill. "We're gonna be sitting ducks if we try to slide down," cried Wally.

Then something happened that was so strange that, ever afterward, Andy said it was proof that miracles still happen. A low cloud dropped down from nowhere and produced a downpour so hard and fast it concealed the two fleeing Americans. They slid all the way down the side of the hill under its cover.

As they reached the bottom, the rain stopped almost as suddenly as it had begun. They looked back up the mountain and saw the Germans staring down at them. Then from somewhere among the rocks in the distance, they heard Frisco open up with his machine gun, and Wally saw one of the Germans drop.

The two evaders, now in officially neutral territory, didn't stick around to see what else might happen. They sprinted away as fast as Andy's wounded leg would allow, down the road stretching out in front of them.[1]

CHAPTER 36

SWISS SURPRISE:
GEORGE STARKS

As soon as Dr. Charlin entered the house, Maurice motioned for George to come with him to the basement. The owners of the house, a man and his wife, followed close behind with their twelve-year-old son, whose face had the eager look of excitement and adventure. George wondered what role, if any, he would play.

The Frenchmen stood together talking rapidly. George gathered they would not be at the house very long. "It must be urgent that we leave here as soon as possible," he thought to himself.

After a few minutes of animated conversation, Maurice explained to George that the young boy would go check things out and return. "Can he possibly be involved with this also?" George wondered about this child, who would contribute perhaps the most important piece of information for his escape into Switzerland.

They all huddled around the basement door of the house, which looked out over a small field. In the distance the tree line suggested a small stream. Maurice explained it marked the border between France and Switzerland. George was literally looking at his freedom.

After speaking urgently to the lad for several minutes, Maurice opened the door, and the boy ran out into the snowy afternoon toward the stream. He disappeared into the trees for several minutes and then could be seen running back toward the house.

Maurice told George to be ready. If the boy saw no German patrols, they would make a run for it. The boy came back breathing hard. "Oui, monsieur, oui!" he said with excitement. It was time.

George Starks

Maurice and I headed out of the house and bolted down that slope like a couple of jackrabbits. We leaped the brook that divided the countries and kept running over the Swiss field until we reached the outskirts of Vallorbe, about a kilometer inside the border. We were across.

Maurice stopped us just short of the town. He was in the country illegally, of course, and I had to continue on alone. He pointed to the Swiss police station, where I was supposed to turn myself in. We stood there a moment more, saying our farewells. For we both thought then, that our times of occupied France and escaping German patrols were over.

I walked on alone over Switzerland's neutral ground—or so I thought—thinking the ordeal was finally past.

When I walked into the police station to turn myself over, they weren't thrilled to see me. They began an intensive interrogation and confiscated my escape kit. When they led me under guard to a small café for dinner that night, they made me pay out of my escape-kit money. The French had never let me pay them for anything, though I had tried.

Then they tossed me into a dungeon-like cell below the ground with only a straw-filled tick and chamber pot for the night's comfort.

The next day the police chief handcuffed me and took me by train to the Swiss military base. Those guys there wanted to shave my head and dust me down for lice.

I wouldn't have it. I mean I raised holy hell. I told them I was an American officer and I wouldn't be treated that way. Anyway I raised Cain and won out.

I took a shower—I wanted that. But I didn't let them shave my head or put any of that dust on me. Next they marched me at rifle point the seven kilometers to the military quarantine camp. For being a neutral country, Switzerland didn't seem too neutral to me.

The quarantine camp was a mess. The Germans more or less dictated the terms of neutrality to the Swiss, and they would keep downed Allied airmen in custody for two weeks so that any military information they might have picked up in occupied France would be outdated.

The camp was located on an old farmstead with the house occupied as an office, and those of us being quarantined were kept in the barn. There was an assortment of Allied airmen in the barn when I got there, all with shaved heads, only straw to sleep on, no clean clothing, no soap or towels or toothbrushes. I began to raise a ruckus and kept raising it.[1]

One morning after George had been there a few days, he looked up to see three familiar faces. "Well, look who's here. If it's not our pilot!" said one of the men. To George's amazement, there stood Don Edgerly, Bill Wyatt, and Bob Williams in the doorway. The three men rushed over to George, slapping him on the back and shaking his hand.

"Well, you no-good son-of-a-guns!" said George. "How'd you get here?" They shared the story of how they had met up in the Lambert residence, where the couple had helped them get clothes and papers, and then begun their walk together to the border. Fortunately, they told George, they were discovered by the French Resistance, who helped them get across.

Then George told them about the men and women who had helped him and recounted his many close calls on his trek through France. His crewmen were amazed as he told them of helping the soldiers with the coffin, the bicycle, and his other encounters with Germans.

"How are things here?" Don asked his pilot.

"Deplorable," answered George. "We've only got straw to sleep on, no clean clothing, or soap, or towels. Nothing."

"What about food?" asked Bob.

"There's not much—a few potatoes and some thin soup," George told him.

"Why hasn't the American legation done something?" asked Bill.

"I don't know," George said. "I'm not even sure they know how bad things are."

George was thrilled to know that at least three of his men had made it safely out of France. But seeing some of his crew again—with shaved heads—made him even more determined to procure better treatment for all of them. He told the guards that he wanted to speak to someone in charge. He kept up his campaign of complaints about the conditions but to no avail. None of the Swiss officials seemed interested. At one point, he tried to get a letter out to the American legation but wasn't certain it was ever sent.

After a couple of weeks, he noticed one morning that the office near the barn was unattended. He looked around and saw no guards. He decided to chance it. Having picked up some of the language, George went inside and placed a phone call to the American embassy. They were astonished when he told them about the treatment they were receiving. At the end of his rant, they said they would handle it.

George hung up the phone and returned to his buddies. "Don't have any idea if that will help or not, but it sure felt good to get that off my chest," he said.

The next morning, as they stood around the yard, George looked up to see the most amazing sight. A long, shiny, black Cadillac with American flags flying on the front bumpers slowly pulled up the road heading for the large barn. The evaders all gathered around the car. Two men from the American legation got out and opened the cavernous trunk, which was filled with Red Cross packages—toilet kits, sweaters, socks, blankets, canned food, and snacks.

George asked the attaché about their status. "Look," he told George, "we're working on getting you guys out early. Just hold fast." It was great news.

In a few days, all the Allied soldiers except George were picked up and taken to Bern. The Swiss detained George for another week—he suspected they considered him a "troublemaker"—before releasing him to the American embassy in Bern.[2]

CHAPTER 37

ENOUGH OF SWITZERLAND: BILL WYATT, BOB WILLIAMS, DON EDGERLY

Bill Wyatt

April 27, 1944

The four of us left for Bern and arrived shortly before noon, when we were turned over to our Legation. That day they bought us a complete outfit of new clothes, and we stayed at the Hotel Baun, which was not bad at all. We were given some money and had a nice time in Bern for three days. I think I would have liked to stay there.

May 1, 1944

We caught the five p.m. train to Montreux, where we are now staying. We are living at the Hotel des Alpes. The train was full of other Americans who were coming from Klosters, where they had spent the winter. Klosters is noted for its skiing, and one American had a broken leg.

We arrived in Montreux that evening and took the funicular to Glion. It is a very small village with about four stores and a barbershop all on one street. We all expected to have some fun here, but ever since we arrived it's been one restriction after another. No one is allowed to go swimming or boating. The Swiss have made it clear that anyone caught trying to return to the war front will be caught and placed in jail.

At night we try to find things to do—there are some films we can go see, and there are several nightclubs and a casino, the Perroquet. Since there's not much else to do, I spend practically all my time at the casino. Once I met a lovely girl there, a dancer, who now dances at Interlaken.

I have met an awful lot of swell fellows here at the hotel. There are quite a number from Philadelphia and Pittsburgh. When I came here four months ago, there were sixty-three Americans. Since then new fellows have been coming in and there are now just a little over a hundred.

There are about fifteen of the sergeants that have been made MPs here. My radio operator, Bob Williams, and I are on duty together with one other fellow. It is a very poor job, because none of us want to turn anybody in. So far I haven't, and I don't intend to at any time. We start at 9:00 p.m. At 11:30 p.m., one fellow goes home and the other two stay on the job until 4:00 a.m. I'm glad we only have to go on duty about once every five days.

June 6, 1944

The Allies invaded France, landing on the Cherbourg Peninsula. It was a very happy day for us here at the hotel. I can imagine how the French people felt. Many times while we were in France trying to get to Switzerland, people would ask us when the Americans were coming. We would say, "Two or three months." They would just shrug their shoulders and smile, as if to say, "I hope you are right." President Roosevelt, I think, is loved by France, as all Americans are. We were told by a woman we met once, who spoke very good English because she had been born in England, that the French no longer had any faith left in the English.

August 18, 1944

Today we learned the Allies are only fifteen miles from Paris. As yet the British have not broken through the Caen area, but it shouldn't be long before they do. We have a map in the hotel lobby, and as we move on, we pinpoint the map. Things certainly look good for us. We are all only waiting for the day we can get out of here and back home. We have had too much of Switzerland.[1]

CHAPTER 38

ROWBOAT RIDE
AT MIDNIGHT:
GEORGE STARKS CONT'D

When George was finally allowed to go to Bern, U.S. officials debriefed him for several days. He shared with them as much as he could remember about what he had seen of troop movements, bases, methods of travel, and those who had helped him escape.

The American legation placed all of the downed flyers, about forty-five of them, in hotels in Bern. George and the other three crewmen from his B-17 found themselves in nice accommodations, and a payroll that finally caught up with them. Civilian clothes were provided, and the young men were free to move about.

These Americans were classified as war refugees. They were free to come and go with one firm condition: they must remain in Switzerland. If a soldier attempted to leave the country and was caught, he would be imprisoned.

After staying in Bern for a few weeks, many of these men, including George and his crewmen, were moved to a hotel in a ski resort area near

Montreux. Here the flyers spent most of their days sitting around or playing tennis, sometimes hiking.

Many of the men encountered girls eager to meet American servicemen. There were also some displaced aristocratic ladies waiting in Switzerland for the war to be over. George met a countess who had fled from Italy and was living in a rented villa. After having lunch with her a couple of times, he was invited to be her guest for the weekend at her villa.

The sprawling complex with tennis courts and a swimming pool was located on a flat ridge overlooking the Alps. The countess had a small contingent of servants and entertained servicemen frequently. One night, after all the festivities were over and the other guests had departed, George found himself in his room suddenly famished for a midnight snack. He decided to tiptoe down to the kitchen and see if there was anything in the icebox.

As he rounded the corner in the darkness, he saw the door to the refrigerator was open and underneath the door he could see a man's bare feet, his upper body bent into the fridge. As he came around the door, he recognized the man as one of the other American flyers who had evaded into the country.

"What in the world are you doing here?" chuckled George.

"Well, I could ask you the same thing," his buddy said back.

"I'm here spending the weekend with the countess," said George.

"And I'm here in the small apartment next door with a baroness," his friend grinned. They both laughed and together looked for something to eat.

As the days wore on, news came that the Allies had established a southern beachhead on the Mediterranean near Marseille. One night at a café, George talked to another B-17 pilot, Harold "Buzz" Killian, about trying to escape from Switzerland and rejoining the Allies moving northward. "I can't stay here any longer," said George. "I don't want to spend the rest of the war on my backside, and maybe if I get back they'll let me continue flying in the war."

"Yeah, but how do we get out? They've got as many patrols on this side as the Germans do on the other side," said Buzz.

"I think I know who can help us," said George. "There was a Frenchman who works with the Resistance, who comes in and out of Switzerland all the time and gives information to British and American intelligence. He helped me escape France. Maybe he can help me get back, now that the Allies are closer. I'll let you know what I find out."

Maurice Baverel had told George that if he ever needed him, to go to a certain café in Lausanne and ask for "Victor," his undercover name. So George took the train to Lausanne and began looking for the café Maurice had told him about. He sat down at an outdoor table and ordered coffee. When the waiter came back with his cup, George told him he was looking for a friend of his named Victor.

"No. There's no one here by that name," said the waiter. George said he understood but that he planned to come back to the café later in the afternoon all the same. He spent a couple of hours walking around and eventually returned to the café. He had been seated only a short time when someone approached him from behind. "Well," said a familiar voice, "what do you want, George?"

The young pilot looked up at the man standing beside him. It was Maurice himself, who pulled out a chair and sat down. "Man, it's good to see you again," said George, delighted to be with this confident and dedicated spy once more. Maurice grinned at George, who explained what had been happening for the past few weeks and why he had wanted to get in touch with him. "I've got to get out of here," he said. "I've played tennis with enough countesses to last a lifetime!"

"Oh, but you should like that," said Maurice, giving George a knowing wink.

"Well, it was okay for a while," laughed George, "but now I really want to try to rejoin the Allies. There are two others who want to try to get back into France too." Buzz Killian and another American pilot had told George that they were also willing to risk crossing. "We hear the Allies are moving closer and closer," added George.

"That's true," said Maurice, "but it will still be dangerous. The border is patrolled heavily as always, and the Swiss are guarding all exits. The only way is to go back across Lake Geneva."

"I'm ready," said George. "And so are the two other flyers I mentioned. When can we go?"

"Let me see what I can work out," said Maurice. "Meet me here tomorrow."

The next day George returned to the café at the appointed time. Maurice had a teenager with him, whom he introduced only as Alex his nephew. Then they went over Maurice's plans.

"I have a Swiss friend who will let us 'steal' his boat. We will row the nine kilometers across Lake Geneva to France. But there's a problem. The border runs right down the middle of the lake. Swiss patrol boats on one side of the midpoint, German patrol boats on the other side. We will need to wait for the best possible condition."

George Starks

Our opportunity soon came—a night storm. By that time the two other airmen knew for sure they wanted to try to escape too. They were not the airmen from my crew but three other pilots who felt they still might be able to fly during the final days of the war. And Maurice brought with him the young man he had introduced as his nephew Alex.

So late that stormy night the five of us made our way to the waterfront of Lake Geneva. We cut the chain of the fifteen-foot rowboat belonging to Maurice's friend and pushed out into the wind and pouring rain. There was low fog and the waves were tossing—a really ugly night.

It was about nine o'clock when we started rowing out toward the middle of the lake. We were all drenched by now and could barely see where we were going. Then suddenly Maurice spotted a searchlight at a distance. He quickly motioned for all of us to duck down into the bottom of the boat.

It was not a moment too soon, because the light swept very close to the boat. After they passed, Maurice said it had been a Swiss patrol. They continued to row. The wind grew stronger and visibility was very poor, which may have been the reason that German patrols never spotted us.

When we finally made landfall around one or two o'clock, we were very near the small French town of Évian-les-Bains. Maurice hid all five of us in a small inlet on the beach and told us to stay put until he could scout things out.

Later that morning, he returned. German troops had already cleared out ahead of the advancing American army.

"George, I think you and the others will be safe to start walking. I think you will run into your troops coming up from the south," Maurice explained.

I shook his hand, thinking this was the bravest, gutsiest man I had ever met. "Maurice, thank you for everything."

"Get going, mon ami!" said Maurice. The friends parted for the final time during the war.[1]

PART V

GOING HOME

CHAPTER 39

GEORGE STARKS AND
THE GREEN HORNET

After Maurice and I said our good-byes we began to walk, and I saw American soldiers going through some woods. It was an advance infantry patrol with a half-track ammunition carrier and a six-by-six truck.

An infantry fellow challenged me with his rifle, and I stuck my hands in the air and explained who I was. They began passing me rearward toward southern Allied headquarters with interrogations at every point, but I didn't mind.

I ended up at a P-47 outfit flying off a turf strip near the beach by Marseille. Then they loaded me on a B-25 that they had borrowed or stolen and flew me to Fifteenth Air Corps headquarters in Foggia, Italy. From there Air Transport Command flew me to Naples, across to Algiers, then RONS[1] to Oran, Casablanca, and from there to my base in England.

Back at Podington, Buzz Killian and I gave instructions to pilots on escape procedures. Then they sent us back to the States, because a pilot was not allowed to fly again in the theater in which he had been shot down. We crossed the Atlantic on a converted Italian liner, MS Saturnia, which was loaded with wounded and a few evaders.

The rest of the war I spent as a mission pilot in Sebring, Florida. Then the war ended…and my ordeal was finally over. I wondered if I would ever see again any of the men, women, and children who had risked everything to help me escape out of France, especially Maurice.

But now, with my face pointed toward home, I began to think more and more about the cute little majorette, Betty Jo. Through a letter from her, I knew she was attending college in Kentucky.

After about a week, the ship finally arrived in New York, then I went by bus to Fort Dix in New Jersey and was given thirty days' leave. I went back home to Florida but stopped in Jacksonville to visit Betty Jo's parents—she was away at school. It sure was good to see them, and they treated me great when I arrived.

When I got home, I needed some transportation, so I asked around and found out there were a couple of Harley-Davidson Police Specials for sale in Orlando. I went and bought one—green with "City of Orlando" painted in gold on the sides—and dubbed it the Green Hornet. My orders were to Miami, and Jo finally came home to Jacksonville. I burned the roads back and forth seeing her.

Two years later, after she finished college and I was in my second year of dental school, I finally married that cute little majorette from Live Oak.[2]

CHAPTER 40

IRV BAUM AND TED BADDER

Irv Baum

On May 31, we boarded ships that took us from England to New York. It was unbelievable to know we were finally headed home. On the transatlantic crossing, lots of the guys just stayed out on the decks, lounging around enjoying the sunshine and watching the ocean roll by.

We arrived in New York on June 6, 1945. I gathered all my belongings and made my way to the bus terminal. It was filled with servicemen checking schedules and making arrangements. We all spoke to each other, but really each man was just interested in his own plans, seeing his family and friends at last.

My bus arrived in Monticello on June 8. I got out and called my mother to tell her I had arrived and would be home shortly. She said to me, "I have just one question, do you have both arms and legs?"

"Yes, Mom," I told her, and then she said, "Well, you get home right now."

That night I began telling my parents everything that had happened. I told them about going to Dachau and helping the Red Cross sort through the bodies. They both teared up, and none of us could really believe it.

I asked about my father's sister, and he became overwhelmed with emotion. She and her family lived in eastern Slovakia, and my father had begged them to leave the country and try to get the States.

When he received a card back from her, she simply said, "How can you leave a business?" referring to the clothing store they owned. It was the last communication my father had had from her. As of now, we don't know what happened to them or where they are, even if they are still alive.

After resting for several weeks, I decided to continue on in the Air Force and wound up staying in as a career, retiring in 1972 as a lieutenant colonel and flying with C-54s.

I've thought about the war and our crash and all the events that happened to us more times than you can count. I even read where Padre Mac often preaches in New York City with large crowds in attendance. He certainly was good to listen to in the POW camp, but I'm sure I would rather hear him at St. Patrick's than as a captive in Germany.[1]

When Ted Badder returned home, his young wife, Faye, whom he had married just a few days before he left for England in 1943, was waiting for him back in Texas. They decided to settle closer to his hometown in upstate New York, after which Ted sought employment as an insurance salesman.

A few years later, they had a son, who eventually became a pilot in the United States Army Aviation, carrying on the flying tradition in the Badder family.[2]

CHAPTER 41

DICK MORSE

We had been marching for over two months, but during the last month, the guards gave us more food and Red Cross parcels and were more humane. They could hear Allied artillery in the distance and knew the Day of Judgment was nearing.

But even when our infantry caught up with us, we had no place to go and nothing to do, so we were just sitting around, tired and exhausted. Once again I nearly lost my wristwatch. A British soldier saw it, came up to me, and started to take it off my wrist. I was surprised and said, "I am an American." He said, "Sorry," and he pushed it back on my wrist.

After I'd rested a little, I took off down the road and came to a place where a mess wagon had been set up for the British troops, and the person in charge was just cleaning up. I asked him for some food, and he handed me a loaf of white bread that tasted so good and had such fine texture that it reminded me of angel food cake.

I got a ride to the American lines with some British soldiers who had confiscated a German truck, then caught a ride to Brussels and from there was taken to Camp Lucky Strike to await transportation to the U.S.A.

When it was time to return to the United States, the GIs could wait for transportation by plane or leave immediately by ship. I didn't want to wait, so I got on a Liberty ship and in fourteen days arrived in New Jersey. There I was hospitalized for several weeks because of malnutrition, dysentery, and some back and joint injuries.

When I was released, I decided to hitchhike home. After getting several rides, I was picked up by a man who said he was just riding around and that he would take me all the way home. Even when we arrived there, he waited in his car until I was safely inside.

I really liked the Air Force and had planned to make it a career. After eleven years, I came home on a thirty-day leave, planning to re-enlist at the end of my leave. It was during this time I met the most wonderful girl, Priscilla. We hit it off immediately, and it became serious quickly.

During that month, my dad talked to me some about not going back in the service but to stay in Rutland and work in his business. However at the end of my leave, I went to the Air Force office to sign back in and there was a sign on the door saying, "Will be back in fifteen minutes."

Instead of waiting around there, I walked down the street to my father's store, and when I told my dad that I planned to re-enlist, he was really disappointed. We talked a long while about it all, and he finally persuaded me to change my mind. Priscilla and I got married not long afterwards.

In April 1994 a group of fourteen former POWs returned to Stalag Luft IV with their spouses to mark the fiftieth anniversary of its liberation. Polish officials dedicated a monument at the site and held a ceremony to honor the prisoners of war who were held there. I attended along with my wife, Priscilla.

After the ceremony, we walked to the campsite. Although all the buildings had disappeared and trees were growing where they had stood, we located a root cellar. From that location we were able to figure out where our barracks had been.

As I was looking where the kitchen area of my building had been, I saw a small piece of iron lodged in the dirt and wondered what it was. After a little digging, I was able to pull out a small iron pot, which I brought home and we have it near our fireplace.

One of the former POWs who was with us that day said our return to Stalag Luft IV was to replace bad memories with good ones. And that's exactly what it did.[1]

CHAPTER 42

BILL WYATT WITH DON EDGERLY AND BOB WILLIAMS

Well, it is September 13 and we are finally leaving Switzerland, and everyone is certainly happy about it. I feel sorry about some of the fellows having to stay because of debts. After they pay them, they too will leave. We all thought it was rather a dirty trick on the legation's part.

We went by train to the border. There were plenty of Swiss officers and guards around. On the other side were the American officers waiting for us with GI trucks.

There were about seventy in our group. All but twenty-one of us went on to Annecy, while we stayed in the village there and ate our dinner. Then we too went on to Annecy on a French Resistance bus.

We had a wonderful time in that town for about six days. The French were very good to us, and those who didn't know us were a bit skeptical. They had learned their lesson of trusting people.

One night in particular, I and several of my friends had a swell time in a little village just outside of Annecy. We got in with a crowd of Frenchmen, and they went wild. Most of them had had a lot to drink, and we stayed there celebrating with them late into the night.

Almost our whole stay there, however, was in bad weather. If the weather had permitted, we could have left three days earlier. We were all just ready to get back to England.

Finally, on September 19 we took off from the Annecy airfield and flew to London. As we came to the airfield our pictures were taken about a dozen times or more. I was on the first plane with another twenty or so men. We took off in a C-47 at 10:37 a.m. and landed at 2:03 p.m. I saw plenty of evidence of the battle of France on our way over.[1]

CHAPTER 43

ANDY BRENDEN
WITH WALLY TRINDER

Andy Brenden

When we started walking into Spain, it wasn't as easy as Frisco had said it would be. There were forks in the road leading in every direction. We finally decided on this one road leading through a small ravine, and that got us into the town of Lérida in Catalonia.

The Spanish police picked us up and threw us in jail. They obtained medical assistance for my wounded knee. They asked for identification, and we told them we were Americans. We still had our dog tags with us. They wired back to our English base to confirm the identification and received confirmation.

We started on the trip to Barcelona on a bus. We arrived there and were greeted at the American consulate. We received treatment like we had never had in our lives. The Americans believe in doing it up right.

They showed us the city of Barcelona and gave us the best accommodations, food, and even some spending money. We just had a wonderful time while we were there.

Then on to Madrid. The consulate told us that we would be given permission to leave Spain to go to Gibraltar and fly from there back to England. We had a chance to see the fortress that guarded Gibraltar, tremendous protection for the coast.

We returned to England and were never ordered to flying duty again. We had a wonderful experience traveling through England and Ireland. And we briefed new crews that came over. We gave them whatever pointers we could on our evasion and hoped that it might help them.

I got quite alarmed at times when my older brother spoke of me as a hero. That disturbed me because actually I was one of the lucky ones. The real heroes were the ones who made their thirty-five or forty-five missions—they're the real heroes…and then of course, the ones who didn't come back.

When we came back to the United States, I was one happy and thankful young man. If the words came out as I wanted, they would have been these:

So it's home again, and home again, America for me!

My heart is turning home again, and there I long to be.

In the land of youth and freedom beyond the ocean bars,

Where the air is full of sunlight and the flag is full of stars.[1]

CHAPTER 44

DALE BEERY AND WILLIAM WALLACE

The substitute co-pilot for George Starks's B-17—listed in official documents variously as Dale Beery and Dale Berry—returned to the States after being liberated from a prisoner of war camp in Germany. For most of the time he was a POW, he was in Stalag Luft III, where Irv Baum and Ted Badder were held, though in a different compound. In later years, whenever George contacted his other crew members, he continued efforts to locate the substitute co-pilot.

William Wallace, the original co-pilot in George's crew, remained at Podington Base in England while he recovered from his gunshot wound. He eventually flew on several B-17 missions, and when the war was over he returned home to South Dakota.

PART VI

FINDING OLD FRIENDS

CHAPTER 45

RECONNECTING, 1969:
GEORGE STARKS

etty Jo and George, along with Maurice Baverel, drove away from Bronne and toward the small town of Vitry-en-Perthois, the village where Paulin Crete took George after discovering him in the woods shortly after the pilot's airplane had been shot down. Now the trio began to search for the house of Josefa Wilczynska, the Polish woman who was the first helper to allow George to stay in her house. She had lived there with her young daughter, Marie Claire.

George recognized the old church near the center of the village and knew he was near Mme. Wilczynska's house, just across the lane from the church's cemetery. He and Maurice walked up to the door of the modest house and knocked. George felt a sense of excitement laced with anticipation. "Will she still be there?" he wondered.

After a few moments, the door opened, and a short, older woman with a round, amiable face appeared. George immediately recognized her. Here was the same woman who had taken him in the day he was shot down. Maurice explained in French who they were, and as George watched her, her expression reflected the returning memory and her dawning recognition of the visitor.

Hesitantly she asked them to come in. As the significance of the moment began to make itself felt, George reached out to shake her hand, and as she looked him fully in the face, her mouth broke into a huge smile, as if she was reliving the afternoon she had taken in the tired and scared young pilot.

"Mais oui, mais oui," she said, nearly as happy to see him as he was to see her. With Maurice's help, the two began recalling all the details of that day in March 1944, twenty-five years earlier.

"How is your daughter?" George asked, speaking of the eight-year-old girl he remembered. He learned that she was married to the owner of a restaurant in the next town, Vitry-le-François, and had a daughter of her own, now about the age she was when George had met her.

George explained that the purpose of his trip to France was to find as many of the people who had helped him and his crew as he could and thank them. Mme. Wilczynska telephoned her daughter and excitedly explained the situation. Marie Claire asked for all of them to drive the short distance to her house so she could welcome them personally. There George learned that Marie Claire's father, the husband of Josefa, who had been a prisoner of war when George met them, had died several years earlier.

With Maurice translating, George told Marie Claire, "So many people helped me while I was trying to escape, and I never got to thank them properly." While he was speaking, George was overcome with emotion, and so was Betty Jo. They both realized that George's dream was coming true.

"Yes, yes," said Marie Claire. "We will have a celebration!" About that time, her husband, Philippe Gomet, came home from his restaurant next door. "We will host a dinner party there tomorrow evening," he exclaimed. "It will be my pleasure to do this! We will invite the mayor and Paulin Crete, the man who first found you in the woods, and others who were here when you came before."

As thrilled as he was, George continued to keep a secret, the surprises he had in his suitcase.

Marie Claire insisted all three of them stay with her at her house while her husband began making plans for the party the next night. The following day, George met with the mayor of Vitry-en-Perthois and revealed to him the surprise he had brought with him all the way from Orlando, Florida. News of the celebration was posted on local bulletin boards for all the townspeople to see.

After a splendid evening of sightseeing and visiting, it was time for the celebration at the Gomets' restaurant. A local band was there to play, and many who had participated in the war attended, some in their old uniforms. When Paulin Crete arrived, George pumped his hand with excitement, and Crete looked as if he was greeting his oldest and best friend. "Welcome back to France!" said Paulin. "But this time, you don't have Germans chasing you!" Everyone laughed heartily, remembering the American pilot who had looked so very young when they first met him.

Sitting at long tables, the guests enjoyed a feast of roasted veal, potatoes, and soup. The wine flowed freely and so did the conversation. After the meal, the mayor stood and began the toasting and speeches while local journalists snapped pictures.

"Ladies and gentlemen, we are honored to have with us today one of the defenders of our liberty. Dr. George Starks, American aviator who was forced to parachute from a B-17 hit by the enemy as he flew over our village on March 16, 1944, and was discovered by M. Paulin Crete and hidden by Mme. Josefa Wilczynska.

"It is to them he returns today, and it is a pleasure for us to receive this valiant soldier. And he brings with him the honor of a certificate making M. Crete and Mme. Wilczynska honorary citizens of Orlando, Florida," said the mayor proudly.

Everyone applauded, and Paulin and Josefa could hardly believe what they were hearing. The courageous Polish woman who herself had endured so much during the war turned to George, and they embraced each other.

The mayor continued. "We congratulate them for him and for the community on which this great distinction falls. And I am very happy to deliver in the presence of Dr. Starks, the diplomas of honorary citizenship of Orlando, Florida." Picking up two parcels from the table, the mayor continued, "And here are their brass keys to the city of Orlando from that city's mayor, Carl P. Langford!"

Everyone cheered and admired the large, shiny brass keys representing their new honorary citizenship. Josefa was overcome with emotion by this time, and so were George and his wife.

"I lift my glass," said the mayor, "in honor of Mme. Wilczynska, M. Crete, Dr. Starks, the United States, and France!"

The dining hall was filled with merriment. As the champagne flowed, the people who a quarter-century before had, in muted and anxious conversations, risked everything to help a young man unknown to them and running for his life now joined with him in uninhibited celebration of their friendship.

As the party wound down and guests began to leave, George pulled out a map of France and spread it on the table. He and Josefa began to retrace his dangerous wartime journey to Switzerland. Josefa glowed with pleasure as she helped him mark possible places he had stopped. George knew the next few days would be some of the most satisfying of his life, and he hoped to find many others who had helped him during his hours of need so many years before.

CHAPTER 46

ON TO PONTARLIER:
GEORGE STARKS CONT'D

The jubilation George felt when he finally said good-bye to the people in Vitry-en-Perthois and Vitry-le-François solidified his determination to find as many as possible of those who had helped him or any of his crew during the war. He decided to drive a short distance to the northeast to Vavray-le-Grand to look for the Lambert family, who had hidden his crewmen Bill Wyatt, Don Edgerly, and Bob Williams for a couple of days after they had parachuted down. It was a long shot, George knew, but he was so elated after finding Josefa and Paulin that he knew he had to try.

The next day George and Betty Jo and Maurice set out, passing once again beautiful fields dotted with wild flowers. In Vavray-le-Grand, Maurice stopped at a café, where they took a table near the window and ordered refreshments. Maurice asked the waitress if she knew the Lamberts. "Yes, certainly," she replied to him in French. "The older Lambert is no long living, but his son and wife remain in the family house." She gave directions to Maurice.

After they finished their rolls and coffee, George was eager to start out once more. "I am so glad to be doing this," he thought to himself. "These people were so good to all of us. And they didn't even know who we were really."

They found the Lamberts' small and picturesque farmhouse just outside the town center. Again, Maurice took the lead and knocked at the door. A handsome gentleman in his late thirties or early forties, too young to have been the owner of the house during the war, answered the door. When Maurice explained their mission to locate the Lamberts, the man's face lit up. "Yes, yes. Of course, I remember them well. My name is Pierre. I am the son of Gérard Lambert, and I remember my mother and father allowing them to stay with us. My parents are no longer living. But come in, come in. I want to show you something."

Pierre Lambert brought George, Betty Jo, and Maurice into a small parlor with a fireplace. "Your crewmates loved this fireplace. Here, sit down," he said, and then he quickly left the room. When he returned, he held a small envelope.

"Look," he said to George, handing him the contents. They were the pictures of his crewmates Don Edgerly, Bill Wyatt, and Bob Williams that they had in their survival kits. The Lamberts had duplicated them twenty-five years before so papers could be drawn up for the young men to aid their passage to Switzerland.

"My father kept these to remember them," he said, smiling broadly at George, who passed the pictures to Betty Jo and Maurice. The photos affirmed they were at the right house.

"This is just tremendous," said George to Pierre. "Do you remember them yourself?"

"But of course—I was twelve years old when they came," explained Pierre. "They taught me lots of English words. One of them also taught me about baseball. It was wonderful to be with them. This one," said

Pierre, pointing to Edgerly, "was very funny. Right here in this very room in front of this fireplace. Of course, I knew the danger my family was taking, but we didn't think about that too much." The Lamberts were thrilled to meet him and know that all ten of his crew members had made it home alive.

After hugs and promises to keep in touch, George, his wife, and Maurice departed. Now he hoped to find the chief of police and his lovely daughter who allowed him to stay at their house for several days and who introduced him to Maurice.

As they set out from Vavray-le-Grand for Pontarlier, George wondered how he ever traveled as far as he did on that rusty bicycle.

After stopping overnight in a hostel, Maurice drove on to Pontarlier, close to the Jura Mountains, the subalpine range that traces much of the border between France and Switzerland. It was here Maurice first laid eyes on the skinny American pilot who looked no more than sixteen at the time. It was also here that the chief of police, Henri Chambelland, had allowed George to stay with him and his pretty daughter, Giselle, for several days.

The town looked nearly the same except that the trees were taller and fuller. George and Maurice had no problem finding the building that had been police headquarters. From the street, it looked as if the upper floors remained occupied. With Betty Jo, they climbed the stairs to the second story and knocked on the door. A distinguished looking gentleman answered, and he and Maurice knew each other immediately.

"My old friend," Henri Chambelland said to Maurice, kissing him on both cheeks. "Come in. What brings this pleasure to my door?"

Maurice turned and introduced George. "Do you remember this man? You hid him for several days during the war, and now he has come back to us!"

The old chief of police could hardly believe it. "But of course. And who is this?" Attention turned to Betty Jo, whose eyes were twinkling. "Yes, and I think you had a daughter named Giselle," she said with a grin. "I've heard about her from George."

"Indeed. I still do. She is married to a doctor now," he told them.

"Well, George is a doctor now too, a dentist!" said Betty Jo. They all enjoyed sharing the news of what had happened to them since the war, and soon Maurice said they must have a dinner somewhere, because George had something he wanted to present.

That evening, a dozen or so people gathered at a restaurant to share war stories and remember the times when so many of them had helped young Americans. At the height of the festivities, George had the pleasure of presenting a key to the city of Orlando to the former chief of police of Pontarlier, Henri Chambelland, and giving him the proclamation making him an honorary citizen.

George had hoped Giselle might be able to attend the dinner party, but she lived in another town. He regretted not being able to see the girl who had taken care of him, but he delighted in hearing about her from M. Chambelland. The celebration, which continued well into the night, was a complete success, filled with both laughter and tears.[1]

CHAPTER 47

THE BOILLOTS
AND DR. CHARLIN:
GEORGE STARKS CONT'D

The next morning, it was time to leave Pontarlier and drive to nearby Les Hôpitaux-Neufs, a few miles from the Swiss border, to see Henri and Nanny Boillot and the brave Dr. Charlin. Maurice had alerted them about the visit, and George could hardly wait to see them.

As they drove along, he recalled his journey on foot up and down these steep hills through the snow. "I must have been either really young or really scared," he said to Maurice, who laughed back at him. And each day Betty Jo grew in her appreciation for what George had endured.

The village at the foot of the Jura Mountains had changed little in the two and a half decades since George had first seen it—a few more houses, perhaps, but for the most part much the same. Cattle and sheep still grazed on the surrounding hills, and to the east rose high, rugged mountains, their tops and passes covered with snow nearly year-round.

When Maurice pulled up to his uncle's house, George bounded out of the Volkswagen and up the steps. Knocking on the door, he soon found himself face to face with Henri Boillot again. "Mon ami, mon ami," said the aging Frenchman, taking George into his arms while Nanny waited her turn to hug their former guest.

"Oh, George, it is so good to see you again," she exclaimed, kissing him on both cheeks. "Welcome back!" George's eyes filled with tears. It was an overwhelming moment for all of them. The Boillots then embraced Betty Jo and invited them in. Maurice quietly slipped into the cozy living room and settled into his favorite chair.

"Do you remember these rooms?" Henri asked George.

"Oh yes, I remember it all. In some ways it seems like yesterday when I was here—looking out these windows down at the Germans riding by in their trucks and on their motorcycles! I was always afraid of getting caught and getting you in trouble," said George, remembering how he had often wondered if he would ever see America again.

George examined several small watercolor landscapes hanging on the wall. "I see you are still painting, Henri," he said.

"Yes, I still enjoy it very much," said Henri. "Here," he said to George, "pick out two of my paintings to take back to the United States."

"Oh, Henri, that would be wonderful," said George. "They will be something we can hang in our home to remember you and Nanny always!"

As George and Betty Jo looked at Henri's paintings, Maurice and his uncle began to plan a reception for George and his wife with the mayor and others in the area. "We will need to contact Dr. Charlin immediately," said Maurice. "There will be others who were with the Resistance who will want to come too." They decided to wait until they arrived at Dr. Charlin's home on the edge of the village of Jougne to have the party.

As the afternoon began to fade, Nanny and Betty Jo set the table for supper, while Henri poured George and Maurice a glass of wine. Henri asked George how much he knew about what Maurice had done during the war. "Well, I knew he had worked with the Resistance and British intelligence throughout the war," said George, remembering some of what Maurice had told him before.

"By the end of the war, my nephew had helped literally dozens of people trying to reach Switzerland. Most of them could ski, however," grinned Henri with a sideways glance at George. They all laughed together, remembering the Florida boy's frustrating encounter with Alpine modes of travel!

George learned in more detail about Maurice's missions supplying information about troop movement and installations to British intelligence in Switzerland. Often he had made several trips a week back and forth on skis through mountain passes infrequently patrolled by the Germans, sometimes even skiing at night. George already knew Maurice was fearless, and these stories only confirmed his belief that this was the bravest man he had ever met.

Now Henri Boillot wanted to hear about George's life since he had been their hidden houseguest. "When I returned to Florida, I began dating Jo, and things escalated quickly. We got married and I entered dental school. Next thing I knew, the Korean War broke out, and I went, this time not as a pilot but as a dentist. While there, I landed shortly after our guys invaded at the battle of Inchon. Those were really rough times too," said George.

"When I left for Korea, Betty Jo had just found out she was pregnant with our first child. After the baby was born, the doctors discovered our little daughter had a severe brain defect and wanted to operate immediately. I put in for leave to come home but was not given permission. Betty Jo dealt with all of that by herself. Unfortunately, the operation did not correct the problem—and our daughter is twenty-three years old now but has developed only to about a five-year-old level," explained George.

Henri, old enough to be George's father, listened sympathetically. "Very difficult," he said to George. He asked about other children.

"Now," said George, "we also have three others, two boys and another daughter."

"Well, you should bring them back here to meet us and see where you had your great adventure!" said Henri, his eyes twinkling.

"I will try to do just that," said George.

After supper the Boillots showed George and Betty Jo the bedroom in the attic he had occupied twenty-five years before. "I remember this well," said George, thanking Nanny once more for all she had risked to help him.

"We have another guest room downstairs you could stay in," explained Nanny.

"No, no!" said George. "We'll stay right here where I stayed during the war."

The next morning they drove to Dr. Charlin's house, a large two-story stucco building surrounded by gardens. Maurice explained that it had been in the doctor's family for generations. "He is in poor health now but will be so happy to have you come," he said.

It took Dr. Charlin several minutes to answer the door, and it was clear that the kind and brave gentleman had endured many health problems. He was completely blind now and walked with a cane. But when George reached for his hand, he embraced George with a hearty hug and shook hands with Betty Jo.

As George's wife listened to a new round of stories about the day the doctor had hidden George in the back seat of his car and passed through four German checkpoints, she once more became emotional. She realized that the doctor had helped numerous Jews escape as well as many Americans. "I never did it to be thanked," he said to Betty Jo. "I did it because I thought it was the right thing to do." Despite his poor health, Dr. Charlin had no trouble describing in vivid detail some of his dangerous exploits. After he had helped George cross over into Switzerland, he and Maurice had worked together several more times to get others to safety.

That evening, about two dozen people gathered at a restaurant to celebrate George's return. Dr. Charlin was the first to receive the proc-

lamation of citizenship and the twelve-inch brass key to the city of
Orlando. At last George had one proclamation and key remaining.

"And to my dear friend, Maurice, I have been instructed by Mayor
Carl Langford of Orlando to bestow citizenship upon you and give you
a key to our city of Orlando also." George could see Maurice was surprised and so pleased with the honor. "You are my friend forever, Maurice. I owe my life to you." The two men, separated in age by only a
half-dozen years, embraced as the townspeople, many of whom had their
own wartime stories of helping American servicemen, cheered.

The local newspaper had publicized the celebration in advance,
attracting a surprise visitor—a priest who had been imprisoned with
Maurice in Germany. The night before Maurice had escaped, he had
given his sweater to the priest, who was shivering and suffering from
fever. The two men, who had not seen each other since that night,
embraced with tears of joy.

At one point during the evening, having noticed that Maurice had
stepped out onto the porch behind the restaurant, George and Betty Jo
joined him as he looked out across the mountains he had crossed so many
times during the war transporting people and information. "You probably know these foothills and mountain passes well," George said.

The Frenchman was slow to answer. "Yes, George, so many memories."

As George and Betty Jo drove back to Luxembourg for their flight
home, George reflected on the journey now ending, an experience beyond
his fondest hopes. He had found more of the helpers from the war than
he had imagined possible, and their hospitality had not diminished. He
knew they would be friends for a lifetime.

CHAPTER 48

BACK WITH MIKE, 1970:
GEORGE STARKS

The following year, 1970, George returned to France to see all his friends again. This time he took his youngest son, Mike, who celebrated his fourteenth birthday there in August.

Maurice took the younger Starks under his wing, just as he had done with his father twenty-six years earlier. But now, instead of looking for a way out of France, they were exploring for something completely different. Early one morning while they were staying at Maurice's parents' house, he summoned Mike: "Let me show you something."

Mike followed him down into the basement. After rummaging around a bit, Maurice found what he was looking for—two tin pails. Handing one to Mike, he said, "Follow me." They headed off through the damp, grassy fields behind the house, down a slight incline toward a trickle of a stream. Maurice stopped and picked up a medium-sized rock. "Look," he said to Mike. Under the rock was a large snail, about the size of a quarter. Maurice pulled the snail off and dropped it into his bucket. He motioned for Mike to begin foraging for snails also.

They spent the better part of two hours turning over rocks, looking along the edges of wide leaves and grass growing close to the water's edge. When their two pails were nearly full of snails of varying sizes, Maurice motioned toward the house and announced, "Time to go back."

Returning to the basement, Maurice opened a narrow wooden trunk. The contents seemed to be alive—and so they were—with snails in what looked like cornmeal. He filled a clean bucket with snails from the trunk then emptied the buckets of snails he and Mike had just collected into the trunk. Closing the lid, he explained to the boy, "They eat the grain, then we can eat them!" Mike was still not sure what he meant.

After retrieving the snails, Maurice took them to his mother in the kitchen, who began cleaning them. Mike watched every step of the process, fascinated. After scrubbing and extracting the snails, Maurice's mother placed a skillet filled with fresh butter and garlic on the hot stove. Once the butter was bubbly, she poured all the snails into the pan and seared them, occasionally testing them with a fork as she went along. "See," she said to her American audience, "these ate cornmeal in trunk—it makes them clean."

Mike was enthralled. He learned later that this process is called "purging," and when snails eat the cornmeal-like substance, it clears them of anything harmful to humans. He couldn't wait to tell his buddies in the States that not only had he collected snails in the garden like hunting for Easter eggs, but he had eaten them also.

That night, spirits were high as the friends visited. George continued to share stories about his family back home and learned more and more about his French family. Maurice was now remarried to a wonderful woman named Paulette. She had known Maurice through her involvement with the Resistance, but they had waited until after the war to pursue their relationship.

"When can you come to visit me in the States?" George asked them. Maurice looked up and smiled. "Mais oui, mon ami! We will come!" George could always count on Maurice to be up for any adventure.

On this second visit, George realized that these people in France would be a part of his life forever. He revisited everyone he could find once again—Marie Claire, the Chambellands, the Boillots, and of course Maurice Baverel. Josefa Wilczynska and Dr. Charlin, however, had died during the year after George's first visit. Josefa and the brave doctor had risked their lives for his sake; he would remember them always, and he was so thankful he had seen them before they passed away.

And it was on this visit that Maurice took George to Paris to see someone very special. "You remember that night we crossed Lake Geneva in the bad storm to get you back to France?" Maurice asked George one morning.

"How could I forget?" said George, grinning. "I was scared to death."

"Well, do you remember that young man I had with me? He was fifteen and a cousin of mine," explained Maurice. "His name is Alex Moussard, and he wishes us to come to see him in Paris!" George remembered only that a young man was with Maurice—a brief introduction had been all the dangerous nature of the mission had allowed. He looked forward to the visit with great anticipation.

Alex Moussard lived in an enormous brick mansion surrounded by gardens near Versailles. An oil executive, he welcomed George and Mike into his home. The three men—Maurice, Alex, and George—recounted in detail their harrowing nighttime escape across Lake Geneva to Mike, who listened in rapt delight, while sipping fizzy water with lemon.

After their visit to Paris, it was time for George and Mike to fly home. George told Maurice, "Just let us know when you want to come visit me in Orlando. Betty Jo and I would love to have you stay with us as long as you wish."

CHAPTER 49

MORE VISITS
WITH FRIENDS

I n 1973, George returned for a third visit to his European friends. This
time Betty Jo and her mother, Louise, accompanied him. There was a
special reason now for celebrating—the wedding of one of Maurice
Baverel's nieces.

The ceremony occurred in a village close to Pontarlier. It was a lovely
spring day, and all the guests walked together along the country lane
from the bride's house to the picturesque church. The reception was held
in a nearby restaurant with a large stone patio outside.

Champagne flowed and guests continued to laugh and dance and
visit until early in the morning. By midnight however, George and Betty
Jo explained to Maurice that they needed to get their mother back to rest.

"These people love life, don't they?" George said to Jo as they walked
back to the house.

"Yes," she laughed. "They certainly do!"

As they strolled along in the lovely evening, George thought to himself how different these times were compared to those moments during the war. By now after three visits, he felt extremely close to all of them.

Before they left France, George had another serious talk with Maurice about coming to Orlando to visit them.

"We will show you a wonderful time. Please try to come," George told Maurice.

"I don't know, George. I'd like to but I'm not sure we can. It is very expensive to fly," Maurice said. The friends departed once more, but George was determined.

In 1977, he sent Maurice and his wife Paulette a gift—funds to help purchase plane tickets for both of them from France to Orlando. The Baverels were finally going to visit the United States and the city where Maurice held honorary citizenship.

The local newspapers covered the visit of one of their adopted sons and Mayor Langford finally met one of the heroes from France, a recipient of a brass key to his city. The city council welcomed the Baverels, and the mayor's office hosted a reception and luncheon afterwards for the visiting hero from France.

The Starks sent the Baverels home with two gifts. Betty Jo had learned that Paulette loved the movie *Gone with the Wind*, so she gave her a tape of the film to take home. "You can practice your English by watching this," Jo said, giving Paulette a big hug. "And you can eat this while you watch it," she said, handing her a large jar of peanut butter, one of Paulette's favorite delicacies.

The following year Maurice and Paulette returned to Orlando, and this time George and Betty Jo drove their friends to New Orleans, a place the French couple had always dreamed of seeing.

Over the years, the Starks continued to stay in touch with nearly all the "helpers" in France who had been instrumental in providing aid to George on his trek to Switzerland. Each exchange of letters and cards only served to solidify their lifelong friendships.

CHAPTER 50

REUNION WITH THE CREW: GEORGE STARKS CONT'D

Several more years passed. George's children grew up, married, and began having children of their own. He had kept in touch with his crew as much as he could. Each of them, like George, had been busy with career and family.

Just as he had wanted to return to France and find the people who had helped him evade Germans, he had a gnawing desire to get together in person with his crew. He had kept in touch with them over the years. But he really wanted to see all of them again—and together. Plans for a crew reunion began to develop.

For most of his former B-17 crewmembers, he had addresses and phone numbers. Most of them had exchanged letters and Christmas cards. But as George poured over the list, he stopped a moment. "I guess as you get older, you want to see the people from your past who were significant," he mused.

As he looked over the names of his crewmen, he began composing a letter to send to the ones he could reach easily. Then he came to the name of his co-pilot on that fateful March day—Lieutenant Dale Beery, a substitute for the regularly assigned co-pilot who had accidentally shot himself in the hand the day before takeoff. But George had been unable to locate him since the war.

George combed through everything he had and made several phone calls into the Michigan area, the last known place of residence for Beery. Then one day, he connected with someone on the phone who actually knew Dale.

"Do you know where he lives now?" George asked. He learned that the former co-pilot had relatives in a town close to his home in Florida. At last he was in possession of a telephone number and called.

George was delighted to hear Dale's voice. He chatted with Beery for a while and invited him to come to their reunion. Dale thanked him and said he would think about it. It was the last phone call George ever had with Beery; he lost touch with him after that.

George typed up the invitation letter, urging his crewmen to come to his house for the reunion. They were now in their late sixties and early seventies with extended families. He told them they could stay with him, or he would make arrangements for them to stay close by. Four of the crew members said they would be there. Three others could not come, and the letter George sent to Bob Williams was returned with no for-warding address.

So in 1987, Irv Baum, Ted Badder, Dick Morse, and Andy Brenden flew to Orlando for a reunion with their pilot. They spent several days together reminiscing about all that had happened to each of them after they crashed and sharing what had happened to them after the war.

The visit sealed their friendships and for a little while, they were all young once more.

ONE MORE TIME TO FRANCE: GEORGE STARKS

2015

P aul Starks, George's oldest son, helped his dad pull their suitcases off the baggage claim at Charles de Gaulle Airport in Paris. For years Paul had heard his mother and younger brother and even his grandmother talk about the people and places they had visited in France, meeting many of the brave souls who had helped his dad and so many others evade the Germans. His mother, Betty Jo, had died a few years before, after a marriage that had lasted more than sixty-six years, and George was now ninety-two. Paul had decided that if he too was going to make that trip, now was the time.

After spending their first day in Paris, they headed for eastern France to the town where it all began, Vitry-en-Perthois, but time had moved on. Josefa Wilczynska and Dr. Charlin had been dead since 1969, and now many members of the Lambert family, Paulin Crete, the Boillots, and others were gone.

The person Paul most regretted not being able to see was Maurice Baverel. Not long after Maurice's second visit to Florida, he had been racing his sports car along a winding mountainous road close to the border between France and Switzerland—his old stomping grounds. No one knew what had happened, but his car was found off an embankment with long skid marks across the pavement. Evidently, he had been going too fast around one of the curves and lost control. Maurice was killed instantly.

As George traveled with his son along the roads that once had been so familiar, his mind turned to his departed friends in France. "They all risked so much for me, everything really," he thought. "Over the years, I'm so glad I was able to reconnect with them."

But now, almost seventy years later, even the roads had begun to look different. George could still recognize major landmarks, but new construction—a building here, houses there—gave each village and town an appearance unlike what he had remembered. Everything seemed to be changing.

They drove the same route as before, beginning in Bronne, where the B-17 had crashed into the field, then on to Vitry-en-Perthois, where George had stayed the first night. George showed Paul the route he had taken out of France. Sometimes Paul would shake his head—after all these years of hearing his dad's story, now he began to really grasp the scope of what he had done.

In Besançon he saw where his dad, on a stolen bicycle, had been stopped by German soldiers and the checkpoint where he should have been arrested. Further on they passed the bakery whose owner had helped George find a guide. Now it seemed to be some sort of apparel shop. Later they drove by the café where the owner had dried his wet clothes on the stove.

Finally they arrived in Les Hôpitaux-Neufs and saw where Henri and Nanny had lived, though the house was now owned by someone else. Paul looked up at the small attic window that had provided his dad's view of the world for nearly two weeks as he watched German troops coming and going in the town below.

Next they arrived in the village where Dr. Charlin had lived. They were able to locate his house, but it looked as if no one lived in it anymore. Many of the flowering vines seemed to be taking over the exterior walls, and some repairs were needed.

"Well, Dad, we may not be able to see any of the people who helped you, but maybe we can find the place where you and Maurice crossed over from France into Switzerland. How about it?" asked Paul.

"Let's do it," said George. Paul headed their rental car toward the border. Once they got to the area where George thought the house had been, where Dr. Charlin had taken him hidden under a blanket and medical supplies, Paul got out of the car and George followed.

"Let's walk down toward that little stream over there," said George as he headed away from the last house in the lane so close to the French-Swiss border.

"After their twelve-year-old boy made sure the coast was clear, Maurice and I came out that basement door back there," said George, pointing back up to the house behind them. "Then we ran like jackrabbits across the field and down into a little opening in the tree line, then across a narrow place in the stream." George's voice filled with excitement and his footsteps quickened.

"Paul, I believe it was right in this area—right about here where we finally crossed over into Switzerland. I remember my heart was pounding, and I knew I couldn't have done it without lots of help, but most of all Maurice's."

Paul followed his dad down to the tree line and could see Switzerland in the distance. He looked around, trying to imagine those momentous events in a world at war, where life and death, risk and reward, formed the substance of each day.

George stopped at the stream's edge. "What a time it was. Thankfully, my entire crew made it after being shot down. Can you believe that? Each of us experiencing so many incredible things—Irv and Ted and our substitute co-pilot in prison, and then Dick, also captured and taken on that Death March; Andy and Wally walking out of France into Spain; then Bill, Don, and Bob meeting up with each other and walking out into Switzerland."

George looked down at the narrow stream and then over into what had been a neutral country during the war.

"And I crossed over about right here, after trekking three hundred miles." George paused and took a deep breath. "I met brave people all along the way fighting to regain their country—so many courageous ones who helped me—some were afraid, of course, and didn't help, but I always understood that. The ones that did—really, they saved my life. What a time it was…what a time."

Paul turned to walk back to the rental car while George lingered by the stream. He suddenly found himself chuckling, as he thought back to the years following his return home. He had decided to stay in the reserves and by mid-summer of 1950 was called to war again, this time in Korea. But he had just completed dental school and would be going as a dentist, not as a B-17 pilot.

"Of all the times," he thought to himself, "Jo was pregnant—it was so hard to leave her. I made the landing at Inchon in an LST shortly after the assault, fell under the command of a gung-ho infantry colonel who was short of field officers," he continued, smiling to himself. He looked up and saw Paul waiting for him in their vehicle.

"But I guess that's a story for another day," he thought to himself as he climbed in, and Paul headed the car back to Paris for the flight home.

ACKNOWLEDGMENTS

To produce a book the scope of this one, many people contributed time and effort. First and foremost my appreciation goes to George Starks: George, you are a true American hero, and I'm so thankful I was able to relive the adventures with you. Sitting around your dining room table listening to your memories of challenge and courage has been a privilege and honor—thank you for your unselfish service and commitment to family, friends, and country. Yours has been a life truly well-lived.

Additional thanks go to the Starks family, especially sons, Paul and Mike, who had already done a tremendous amount of research over the years to add to their dad's collection of memorabilia and information. I appreciate the time you spent with me talking about these stories you grew up hearing and sharing research material.

Next, every family I was able to contact of the original B-17 crew made the enormous task, spanning nearly three years of research, possible. Thanks to all of you: the Badders, the Baums, the Morses, the

Brendens, the Wyatts, and the family of Don Edgerly—for sharing tapes and photos, diaries and journals. These first-person accounts add color and authenticity to the story—wonderful insights into each crew member as well as the people they met along their separate journeys to freedom. They are all heroes—American and French—never to be forgotten.

My sincere thanks next to my agent, Greg Johnson, president of Wordserve Literary and FaithHappenings.com, for appreciating a good war story and then finding the right publisher for this project. Greg, you are the best!

To all the folks at Regnery Publishing: I have thoroughly enjoyed working with each and every one of you. You all have been so gracious to me. Thanks to Alex Novak for taking the manuscript in the first place and to Loren Long and Will Hudson for your contagious enthusiasm and wonderfully creative thinking on how best to present and promote the book. There are others there who touched the project and added their own distinctive input—my gratitude to each of you.

However special thanks must go to the editor at Regnery, Tom Spence, whose discerning red pen respected the work and never compromised the story. Your brilliant editing on the manuscript made me look good—I felt I was back in grad school and loved every minute!

To my wonderful team here in Orlando: to Brenda Holder for reading behind me on each chapter and providing much-needed input. In addition, Bren, I count on your encouragement! You are a true friend and more importantly…a prayer warrior.

Along these lines, many thanks to Jim Wortham for scanning and helping with photos—your work is always wonderful; and to Bret Melvin, whose illustrations add such great dimension and visual information to the text. Hopefully we will have many more projects together.

And of course, last but never least, to my dear husband who always rustles up the greatest gourmet meals during crunch time—there would be no books without you, sweetheart! Thanks for your patience and kindness as I push forward pursuing my dream of recording the biographies of those we need to remember.

Now for a serious moment of reflection…

Ever since I realized the tremendous military heritage in my own family—a father who was a career Chief Petty Officer in the Navy serving through WWII, an uncle who was a line chief for General Claire Lee Chennault in China, a stepfather who entered WWII on the first day of conflict and returned on the last serving in Africa and Italy, and many other relatives as well—I have been interested in military history.

How do we properly thank the men and women who have given themselves to our country? Every story is different; they stir the soul with acts of bravery and unselfish deeds.

I pray that reading stories such as the ones recorded in this book will in some way express gratitude for their service and honor their lives.

And to every man and woman who serves us today in our United States military—you are constantly in our hearts and prayers.

NOTES

CHAPTER 2: BEGINNING AT SIXTEEN

1. Pyote, Texas—Located in far West Texas in Ward County, Pyote at one time boasted a population of more than 3,000 thanks to oil industry activity in the area. In 1942, the military established an air base there primarily to train B-17 crews for the war effort. The influx of so many young servicemen drew numbers of people from surrounding towns, especially on weekends. Its large runways, where once the thundering "heavies" could be heard taking off and landing at all hours of the day and night, are now cracked and overgrown with weeds, a shadowy reminder of days gone by. As of the 2010 census, the population of Pyote, where so many American flyboys got their first taste of what going off to war involved, was 114.

2. Early in the war, the United States entered into a "Lend-Lease" agreement with Great Britain. The United States gave Britain several World War I–era destroyers in exchange for sites where military bases could be built to sustain the war effort. One of these became Goose Air Base, in the

province of Labrador, Canada. By 1941, three 7,000-foot runways had been built, and by 1943, it was the largest airport in the world. Here, airplanes being shuttled to Europe could stop, refuel, and obtain any maintenance required for the remainder of the trip. By September 1945, the base had handled more than 24,000 aircraft within a year.

CHAPTER 3: ONLY ONE JUMP...EVER

1. Affectionately known as the "Pod," Podington began in 1941 as the temporary home to a few Royal Air Force bomber squadrons. Later in 1943 it developed into its primary mission during World War II—the home of the Ninety-Second Bomb Group of the U.S. Army Air Forces. From here, B-17s flew nearly 275 missions during a two-year period, during which 150 aircraft were lost.

2. The large bay known as the Wash cuts deeply into the eastern coastline of England, forming sides at right angles, each side approximately fifteen miles in length. The Wash was more than a hundred miles from RAF Podington, and B-17 crews practiced flying to it, discharging their guns, and flying back. It provided an unpopulated area over which to train in formation flying. Often it was also the last place to fly over before leaving for the continent of Europe when participating in an actual mission.

CHAPTER 4: A WHISTLE SIGNAL

1. George Starks—personal journal and interviews with author.

2. Christopher Clayton Hutton, nicknamed "Clutty," became the Technical Officer to the Escape Department and during World War II was responsible for inventing numerous gadgets used by escaping and evading servicemen. Perhaps his most notable invention was the silk map placed in every airman's survival kit before he went on a mission over Europe. The benefit of silk was that it was noiseless, lightweight, and sturdy. The maps could be crumpled up and hidden in boots or clothing, yet smoothed out flat when needed. Members of the B-17 crews used their silk maps and compasses to guide them as they attempted to evade the enemy.

3. George Starks—personal journal.

CHAPTER 5: BETRAYED BY THE GENDARMES

1.   Ted Badder, taken from video speeches courtesy of the Badder family.

CHAPTER 6: "ARE YOU HEBREW?"

1.   Irv Baum, taken from personal interviews with author.

CHAPTER 7: COGNAC AND EGGS

1.   Dick Morse, edited from personal accounts as told to his wife, Priscilla Morse.

CHAPTER 8: MEETING UP WITH BUDDIES

1.   Bill Wyatt, edited from personal diary courtesy of the Wyatt family.

CHAPTER 9: MEETING IN A SHACK

1.   Arden Brenden, written and edited from original military de-briefings/ reports (E+E 748-750, 1945) after returning to Allied Forces.
2.   Wally Trinder, written and edited from original military de-briefings/ reports (E+E 748-750, 1945) after returning to Allied Forces.

CHAPTER 10: A CASKET AND A BICYCLE

1.   George Starks, personal accounts and interviews with author.

CHAPTER 11: PROCESSING IN FRANKFURT AM MAIN

1.   Frankfurt am Main—The German *Durchgangslager der Luftwaffe*—"air force transit camp"—usually shortened to *Dulag Luft*, was where captured Allied airmen were interrogated, processed, and assigned to prisoner of war camps deep inside Germany. Eventually the word *Dulag* became synonymous with interrogation. Before the Frankfurt *Dulag* opened, thousands of POWs were processed at nearby Oberursel, which closed in September 1943 because of bombing.
2.   Irv Baum, written from personal interviews with author.
3.   Ted Badder, written from recorded interviews courtesy of Badder family.

CHAPTER 12: LIVING WITH THE VIDELS

1.   Dick Morse, written and edited from personal accounts as told to his wife, Priscilla Morse.
2.   Dick Morse, written and edited from personal accounts and journals.

CHAPTER 13: "GET THE HELL OUT OF HERE"

1.   Dick Morse, edited from personal accounts.

CHAPTER 15: AN ENGINEER'S HOME, A DRESS SHOP, AND A ROOT CELLAR

1.   Written and edited from military debriefings and journals.
2.   Ibid.
3.   Ibid.

CHAPTER 16: A SQUEAKY WHEEL

1.   George Starks, personal accounts and interviews with author.

CHAPTER 17: LIFE IN STALAG LUFT III

1.   One of the most well-known POWs at Stalag Luft III. His courageous exploits were well documented even before his capture. After the war he served as minister for various congregations and finally was appointed professor of practical theology at Glasgow University, where he taught and ministered until his retirement in 1984. Padre Mac remained active until his death at ninety in 2004.

CHAPTER 18: 11, RUE DE SAUSSAIES, GESTAPO HEADQUARTERS, PARIS

1.   Dick Morse, written and edited from personal accounts as told to his wife, Priscilla.
2.   This building, a block from the Élysées Palace, was the location of unbridled torture of resistance fighters and other victims. After the war, it was remodeled for the Ministry of the Interior. In 2005, the building was opened to the public. Visitors can see cell walls bearing the patriotic words of resisters, urging prisoners "not to give in."

CHAPTER 19: FRESNES PRISON, PARIS

1. Dick Morse, written and edited from personal accounts.
2. Ibid.

CHAPTER 20: DULAG LUFT AND THE FORTY-AND-EIGHTS

1. Dick Morse, excerpted from personal accounts as told to family.

CHAPTER 21: STALAG LUFT IV, DEEPER INTO GERMANY

1. Stalag Luft IV was one of the most inhumane of the POW camps.
2. Dick Morse, excerpted from personal accounts as told to family.
3. Ibid.

CHAPTER 22: ANGELS WATCHING OVER

1. Bill Wyatt, from his personal diary (edited).

CHAPTER 23: TROOP TRAIN AND A BRAVE MAN

1. Andy Brenden, from personal accounts and debriefings.
2. Personal accounts transcribed from video recordings, courtesy of the Brenden family.
3. Ibid.

CHAPTER 24: THE CAPTAIN

1. Andy Brenden and Wally Trinder, taken from personal accounts.

CHAPTER 25: "FRISCO"

1. Andy Brenden, adapted from personal journal, courtesy of the Brenden family.
2. Taken from personal accounts.

CHAPTER 26: THE THEATER AND THE STRESS OF POW CAMP

1. Known as the "gentleman commandant," von Lindeiner adhered to the Geneva Conventions during his command of Stalag Luft III and gained

the respect of most Allied senior officers. After the execution of the fifty men who had participated in the Great Escape, he feigned mental illness to escape execution himself. After sustaining a wound during battle against the advancing Russians, he surrendered to British forces and was incarcerated for two years in the British prison known as the "London Cage." Later repatriated, he died in 1963 at the age of eighty-two, just a few weeks before the movie *The Great Escape* premiered.

CHAPTER 27: ONE MORE DAY

1.   George Starks, personal accounts and interviews with author.

CHAPTER 30: A TRAIN FULL OF GERMANS

1.   George Starks, personal accounts and interviews with author.

CHAPTER 31: MAVRICE BAVEREL, A SPY FOR ALL SEASONS

1.   According to Baverel's own accounts to the war department, he had personally helped at least a dozen U.S. servicemen get into Switzerland. These, plus dozens of others across Europe who sought to flee from the German occupiers, were among the ones Baverel helped to flee. Sometimes there were even whole families.

2.   George Starks, personal accounts and interviews with author.

CHAPTER 32: DR. CHARLIN AND THE FIVE-HORSEPOWER PEUGEOT

1.   In the book *La ligne de démarcation*, printed in France in 1966, Dr. Charlin provides personal insights into his extensive resistance activities during the war. Not only did he help Starks and other Allied servicemen, but he was instrumental in helping dozens of Jewish families flee into Switzerland.

2.   George Starks, personal accounts and interviews with author.

CHAPTER 34: THE BLACK DEATH MARCH

1.   In an article in *VFW Magazine*, Gary Turban wrote: "Finally in the spring of 1945 the March was over. From beginning to end it spanned eighty-six

days and an estimate of six hundred miles. Many survivors went from 150 to perhaps 90 pounds and suffered injuries and illnesses that plagued them their entire lives. Worst of all, several hundred American soldiers (possibly as many as 1,300) died on this pointless pilgrimage to nowhere. The overall measure of misery remains incalculable. Although often overlooked by history, the death march across Germany ranks as one of the most outrageous cruelties ever committed against American fighting men."

2.   Dick Morse, written and edited from personal accounts as told to his wife, Priscilla.

CHAPTER 35: A SMALL MIRACLE

1.   Andy Brenden and Wally Trinder, from personal accounts recorded by family members.

CHAPTER 36: SWISS SURPRISE

1.   George Starks, personal accounts and interviews with author.
2.   George Starks, personal interviews with author.

CHAPTER 37: ENOUGH OF SWITZERLAND

1.   Bill Wyatt, excerpted and edited from personal diary.

CHAPTER 38: ROWBOAT RIDE AT MIDNIGHT

1.   George Starks, personal accounts and interviews with author.

CHAPTER 39: GEORGE STARKS AND THE GREEN HORNET

1.   "RON": remain overnight. RONs were overnight trips.
2.   George Starks, personal accounts and interviews with author.

CHAPTER 40: IRV BAUM AND TED BADDER

1.   Irv Baum, personal accounts and interviews with author.
2.   Ted Badder, family records.

CHAPTER 41: DICK MORSE

1.   Dick Morse, personal accounts and family records.

CHAPTER 42: BILL WYATT WITH DON EDGERLY AND BOB WILLIAMS

1.   Bill Wyatt, excerpted and edited from personal diary.

CHAPTER 43: ANDY BRENDEN WITH WALLY TRINDER

1.   Andy Brenden, from personal accounts courtesy of the Brenden family
      (quoting "America for Me" by Henry van Dyke).

CHAPTER 46: ON TO PONTARLIER

1.   All material in Chapters 46–51 comes from the author's interviews with
      George Starks and his family.

INDEX

ABOUT THE AUTHORS

Growing up in a family steeped in military history, **CAROLE ENGLE AVRIETT** often heard her uncle—chief mechanic for Claire Chennault's Flying Tigers—insist, "Ain't no fake stories ever gonna outdo the real ones." Convinced that he was right, Avriett pursued a career as an editor with *Southern Living* magazine for nearly fifteen years recording real-life stories, then as an author at the intersection of true-life narratives and military history. *Coffin Corner Boys* is her sixth book.

GEORGE STARKS returned to France many times with his wife and sons, retracing his trek and locating nearly everyone who helped him in his escape. Dr. Starks was actively involved for many years with the National Museum of the Mighty Eighth Air Force in Savannah, Georgia. He spent his retirement in Orlando, Florida, and passed away in 2018.

Also by Carole Engle Avriett

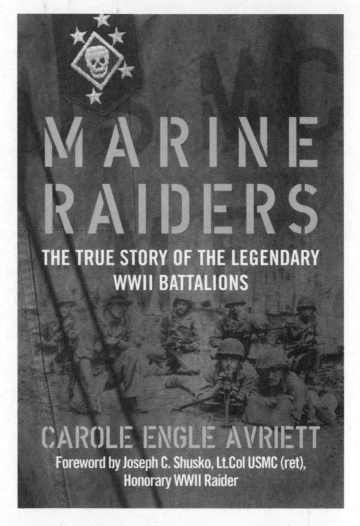

MARINE RAIDERS
THE TRUE STORY OF THE
LEGENDARY WWII BATTALIONS